This couple was ~impressive when they w... ...eir on "The Hour of Power"; a message was somewhat ... well as positive. The book will ... Hopefully, the book will ... more than ordinary. Congratulations Lee Ann and John.

Marion
Augustine

SETTLE FOR MORE

You *Can* Have the Relationship You Always Wanted ... *GUARANTEED!*

Tom Merrill, Ph.D. and
Bobbie Sandoz-Merrill, M.S.W.

SelectBooks, Inc.

This edition published by SelectBooks, Inc. For information address SelectBooks, Inc, New York, New York.

First Edition

ISBN 1-59079-069-3

Library of Congress Cataloging-in-Publication Data

Merrill, Tom, 1940–
  Settle for more : you can have the relationship you always wanted -- guaranteed! / Tom Merrill & Bobbie Sandoz-Merrill. -- 1st ed.
    p. cm.
  ISBN 1-59079-069-3 (alk. paper)
  1. Marriage--United States.   2. Married people--United States--Psychology.
  3. Man-woman relationships--United States.
  I. Sandoz-Merrill, Bobbie, 1940–   II. Title.

HQ536.M42 2005
306.872--dc22

2004024397

Manufactured in the United States of America

10 9 8 7 6 5 4 3 2 1

We dedicate *Settle for More* to each other,
and to our partner, Grace, without whom
this book could not have been created.

Contents

Acknowledgments

All sizeable efforts succeed or fail as a function of the relationships encountered in that effort. This book is no exception. We have been most fortunate and blessed by the relationships that have developed and grown as *Settle for More* grew from concept to completion. We want to acknowledge those relationships.

Our dear friend, Judge Mike Town taught us the Celts believed at certain times in the human experience such as the birth of a child, death, or commitment to another, that God is present in what they called a "thin moment." At such times the veil between the human soul and The Soul becomes almost transparent. As Mike participated in our marriage, it became such a moment. And Pastor Dan Chun married us in that moment. To both Mike and Dan, we are thankful for the relationship that took the risk, the leap of faith that believed we would make it in our determination to have the life partnership we had always wanted.

Barbara Cox Anthony has been unfailing in her support. Her genuine friendship, advice and humor have provided much of the glue in our relationship. Without her, this would be a very different book.

Bill Gladstone, our agent, saw the potential, took a gamble and made a huge hurdle in the process a non-hurdle. Incredibly bright, funny, gentle, and a person of unassailable integrity, he represents the best of this business.

Kenzi Sugihara and his son Kenichi **are** Select Books. Their patience and willingness to go through this process with us side-by-side, sharing their wisdom, knowledge and energy, have put this book in your hands. All authors should be so lucky as to have a Kenzi and a Kenichi publish their work.

Tom Oder, Managing Editor of COXnet/Cox News Service is a newfound friend. A man who does the work of three, he has given his time, humor and friendship generously and freely to edit our column that is distributed by Cox News Service to the 650 clients of the New York Times News Service, including the 17 daily Cox newspapers (A sampling of these are included in the appendix.) One of the joys in writing the column is to hear Tom say, "You hit another one out of the park." His willingness to share his support, his editor's pen and his insights with us have helped to hone our ideas. Of even greater value, he has made it easy to build a friendship with him that we will never forget. Tom is a man who truly settles for more.

Drs. Dick Kappenberg, Craig Robinson, and Bob Spicer, friends and colleagues in psychology, were the first professionals with whom we shared our ideas. Their enthusiastic embracing of the model were both validating and energizing and in their friendship we have seen the model applied in real life.

Our clients/patients and *Settle for More* Seminar participants have enabled us to sharpen the model to its current form. Their collective wisdom, experiences and successes are reflected in the material in the pages that follow.

Maggie Wunsch read our first draft of the manuscript, pulled out her pom poms and cheered us on. It was her comment "once you get the idea of *Settling for More* in your head, nothing will ever be the same" that let us know we were on the right track. Her feedback and support have been invaluable.

Other bright friends and early readers Kathy MacNaughton and Virginia Beckwith's feedback that *Settle for More* was not just life-changing, but world changing let us know we had delivered our message.

All our other friends who have shared and/or endured the excitement of our relationship and the Model that is the basis for this book, have given us the gift of their friendship. For that we are honored and grateful.

And finally, but perhaps most importantly our children, step children, grandchildren and step grandchildren. For they are the ones who give us our reason for being and our hope that we can have it all. We ask that they do nothing less than *Settle for More.*

Our Promise: Dramatic Relationship Success

"In expressing love, we belong among the underdeveloped countries." —SAUL BELLOW

Christine was in tears and Robert was looking somewhat befuddled as she described how they had gone from the magic of a new marriage to one she viewed as having settled into a normal relationship with the usual ups and downs ... then shifting later to a muddle of deceit, lies and tremendous heartache. They had stumbled along in this unhappy state for the sake of the children for a number of years until Christine discovered Robert's affair and confronted him directly. The children were at the age when children leave home. And she thought she might do the same. But Robert protested, and to Christine's surprise, he wanted to save the relationship.

They entered into therapy with the best talent available in Melbourne, Australia and began what was to be a long, painful process in an attempt to salvage their marriage. Nine months later, they sat with us describing what appeared to be a therapeutic failure, with Christine all but packing her bags.

1

We were in Australia on business and to conduct a relationships seminar and had agreed to do some private consulting with Christine and Robert, using our *Relationship* Model. And so, we met together with both of them in two three-hour sessions for a total of six hours.

During our first hour Robert was arguing like the attorney he is, and revealed only how dug into the rightness of his position he was. He was well equipped to wear us out, just as he had Christine over the past thirty years, and the strength of his determination to continue along this fruitless course might have inspired us in our pre-Model days to suggest Christine move forward with the divorce she was considering.

Instead, we interrupted the tedious road Robert had taken in order to explain our Model, and after a few hours of working together with it, we saw a sudden and heartfelt shift in Robert's face accompanied by an equally abrupt change in his viewpoint and conversation.

We knew from our past experience of working with the Model what had happened, and we knew in that moment that Christine and Robert would not only be able to make their relationship work if that's what they wanted, but to make it an expanding and joyful experience.

And we were right. Before long they were tearful, then holding hands and finally laughing and planning a life together. Christine unpacked her bags, and they have since continued on this new, more fulfilling and happier course.

So what happened? What happened during those six hours to so completely transform a troubled, terminal relationship—one that was all but down for the count—to one of hope and optimism for a rich and robust partnership between two people committed to creating and continuing in a relationship? And why did we know it would turn out this way? How could we have predicted it in the face of over half of such marriages failing?

Although we each have many years of effective counseling and consulting experience, neither of us could claim an unusually high success rate in the art of couples' work in our pre-Model days. But since using the Model for the past three years, we have witnessed dramatic turnarounds in almost all of our cases involving partnership.

In fact we saw these results the very first time we used the Model. And because of this completely different outcome, co-counseling with couples has become a specialty in our practice. We also discovered within a few months of developing the Model that it works equally well in helping people in all interpersonal interactions. Our early success was soon followed by invitations to conduct seminars with couples, then schools, churches, businesses and other professionals. The reaction has been the same for most people that it was for Robert and Christine.

We saw from this response that the Model had even wider application and began writing a relationship column which is now carried by the New York Times/Cox News Service List. Next we began to write this book. Our mission evolved into one of helping as many people as possible understand the joy of living this way in their personal partnerships and homes, including their children and beyond ... with friends and colleagues and the rest of the world.

When couples first asked what it is that is so rapidly transforming for people and why, we were unable to give a concise answer. In time, we came to realize that we really can't summarize the Model in a few sentences or paragraphs, but require a few hours or a few hundred pages to convey it. The reason for this is *not* that it's complicated. It's not complicated, nor is it hard to grasp. In fact it's amazingly simple, and easy to understand and use. But it does involve a complete shift in the way you look at things, the same shift we saw on Robert's face and the same shift that had happened earlier for Christine. It's the shift that seems to happen for everyone who is introduced to the Model. And that we can explain.

It is a shift that, once you make it, will change the way you look at everything and serves as the soil for transforming your relationship no matter what state it is in—or even if you are not yet in one—to the partnership of your dreams. In fact, with this shift you are encouraged to then take the lid off and dream even bigger and higher than you have ever done and to create a relationship that is unlimited and expanding ... one that will show you new levels of human possibility.

To begin your dream, imagine what it would be like to have your relationship abundantly filled with love, kindness, support, synergy and joy—and more—every day, all day for the rest of your life. Then know you can have this and more ... and that you can have it now.

This is the promise of the process described in *Settle for More*. It shatters many common myths of marriage, including the one that assumes the initial "rush" and incredible joy found in the early stages of love-relationships can't last. They not only *can* last, they can grow exponentially by using our new, yet simple approaches to replacing the myths.

And so as you now turn the following pages to uncover the secrets of the Model, remember that you too can *Settle for More*. That's the promise we offer ... and that is a guarantee. And when you read the final chapter, you will see that we have the power to rather easily and rapidly *settle for more* in our world as well ... once we begin to do so in our personal lives.

Tom and Bobbie Merrill
Honolulu, Hawaii

"Dreams come true. Without that possibility, nature would not incite us to have them." —JOHN UPDIKE

SECTION 1

Raising the Bar
to Go Beyond
Just Good Enough

ONE

"It Won't Last"

"The easiest kind of a relationship for me is with 10,000 people. The hardest is with one." —JOAN BAEZ

TOM SAYS

"You're noots," she said. "Tag and release," he advised. Words of wisdom from family and friends when I announced I was marrying for a second time.

They had known me through the trials and tribulations of my first marriage, a union that produced three wonderful daughters, provided a platform for me to grow up, and eventually ended due to our "growing apart." My sister and friend were right, I needed to take greater care in going into partnership again, but I wasn't listening.

And so, starry-eyed, I entered undaunted into a disastrous second marriage that wreaked havoc with my career and had me swimming in an emotional and financial Cuisinart. After ten years, I finally extricated myself and returned home to Honolulu to settle into a self-focused, rejuvenating existence with no intention of ever again sharing time and space in the context of an intimate relationship. At age 60, I figured I'd had it.

And then I ran into Bobbie. Literally.

Life was good. I was tucked in early each night and up at 5 am and in the ocean by 5:30, enjoying Hawaii's glorious sunrises from the vantage point of my one-man canoe.

I had just finished a particularly vigorous workout in the water and was running to my car, late for my first appointment. Large cup of coffee in hand, I rounded the corner and ran smack into the woman who had been my eighth grade crush, spilling coffee all over both of us.

"I'm getting divorced," she offered for openers.

"Oh, that's too bad," I said with sincerity, while coolly dabbing at the spilled coffee on my shirt.

"Actually, it's overdue," she said, "since we've been quietly separated for a number of years." And that's how it all started.

She was leaving for a week's trip to California, so we jousted via email and agreed to get together when she returned. We did and the relationship took off like a rocket.

It was a classic whirlwind romance. Late night phone calls. Early morning phone calls. Dinners. Lunches. Breakfasts. Concerts. Movies. Hours of intimate conversation. Pounding hearts when we were together. Concentration problems when we were apart. We had fallen loudly, wonderfully and visibly in love. And it showed. Our friends offered congratulations, along with the unsolicited admonition, "Enjoy it … it won't last."

Why would anyone say that? I knew they were loving, supportive friends who were genuinely happy for us. So I was puzzled. What could their motivation possibly be? Whatever the reason, it brought back pictures of my sister and friend questioning my sanity and waxing wise as I was about to plunge into my second marriage. And it got my attention. This time I wanted to take the care they were suggesting … but I wasn't sure how to do it.

The fact is there have been more self-help books written in the past five years than in the entire history of publishing.

More mental health professionals have been turned out by professional schools over the past decade than during the preceding 100 years. And more people are turning to organized religion in the United States than ever before.

Yet the divorce rate continues to hover above 50 percent for first marriages, 60 percent for second marriages and a cool 78 percent for third tries. And these are only the statistics for marriages. Data indicate that across the spectrum relationships are in trouble.

So, given these numbers, you might think it would make sense for me to pay attention to the warnings of my friends and family. And since I was one of those unfortunate people who contributed to the first and second-time marriage statistics you might assume that "it won't last" would be my own personal mantra. But as Bobbie and I traded stories, we almost simultaneously asked, "Why won't it last?" And then after a brief pause we asked again, "Truthfully, why won't it?"

And so we stopped asking and started looking at the question. Between us, we have over fifty years of experience working with couples in troubled relationships. We have both failed in our own prior marriages. And many of our long-time friends have terminated at least one marriage. The outlook was not promising. And so we openly talked about the risks of marrying again at our stage in life. We concluded that if we were going to make the commitment, we did not want to fail. So we investigated the "Why won't it?" question with new passion and vigor.

BOBBIE SAYS

I had finished tending to the wounds of my failed marriage and after a long separation decided to move on.

During this period, I developed a mild interest in a man from my Honolulu community while listening to him sing with a group of friends one night. He was someone with whom

I had enjoyed a brief flirtation in the eighth grade, but had not thought much about him during the subsequent years as we went our separate ways to finish growing up, marry other people, raise our children and pursue careers in and out of our home state of Hawaii. But now as I thought again of who I might enjoy as my life partner this man came to mind. In fact, he was the only one who came to mind. I had heard he was going through a divorce and was reminded of a wonderful conversation I had enjoyed with him years earlier, a conversation that had revealed a community leader with a good heart and bright mind. And so I put his name on my wish list, placed it in a prayer box, and forgot all about it.

Almost a year later, I was running late to a breakfast gathering of girlfriends. As I scurried from the parking lot up the stairs to the club where my friends were meeting, I saw this attractive man bounding toward me with his face twinkling and eyes dancing from behind his tinted glasses. As he drew closer and our eyes met for a moment, I could see both the eighth grader and the grandfather at once, and without warning my heart leaped to my throat.

In the next moment we bumped into each other—literally, and as I worked to regain my composure, he brushed at the coffee I had spilled on his clothing. I asked about his marital status, and shared the news of my divorce.

He screwed up his face to express his regrets, but he could see from my response that the time was right for me to take this step. And so he let go of his concern and suggested we meet for lunch. We talked briefly and then continued on our separate ways. I called out my email address as he walked toward his car, and noting a lightness in his smile as he repeated it back to me, I sensed his interest might be equal to my own.

I continued somewhat shaken along the path to my breakfast meeting and was reminded by a wave of chills running down my spine of the earlier request I had placed with the Universe.

When I joined my girlfriends at their table looking out over the ocean, I flopped into my chair and whispered, "Oh my God!" I then announced that I had run into "Tommy" Merrill, referring to him by the name we had called him in junior high. They looked a bit puzzled and, without paying much attention to my random declaration, shifted the subject back to other things.

I didn't know why I felt so strongly that this particular man would be part of a truly wonderful period already underway in my life, or why I felt so immediately at home with him, but the answers came in the following weeks as we fell head over heels in love. This unexpected yet dizzying romance took us into uncharted territory that included gratifying conversation, deep emotional connection, hours of laughter and an overall sense of security and joy.

This wonderful encounter came at a particularly good time in my life, and I embraced it greedily. My sister knew more than anyone else what a blessing it was for me, so I was shocked when her response to my good news was a warning to, "Enjoy it, because it won't last."

I faltered through the remainder of our conversation and hung up the phone feeling dejected by her reaction. Why would she suggest that I brace myself for the end of a love affair that had just begun? Others had also suggested this inevitability, and some even seemed impatient for us to get over it and return to our routines with them. Tommy overheard this conversation with my sister and put his arms around me as I fussed about people telling us to get over it. He had been hearing similar comments, and observed how common this response is to people in love. He also noted how well it reflects our cultural expectation that intense love can't possibly last and must be expected to eventually die.

He then suggested we not conform to this self-defeating cultural standard, but instead "raise the bar" on our personal standard of possibilities for partnership. And so rather than passively *settle for less* and allow our love to fade, we decided to *Settle for More* and actively engage in keeping it dynamic and alive.

WE SAY

Studies have shown that a supportive, loving partnership is the thing people most value and want in their lives. And yes, the majority of us want the rest of it too—the great career, the successful children, security, health, money, and the good life— but when we dig below the surface and look at what makes our lives worthwhile, we ultimately come back to our desire for a fulfilling primary partner in the context of a supportive, loving relationship.

Culturally the value of partnership in general, and specifically marriage, has such strong historic and social support that movie plots are built on this goal, soap operas and novels revolve around its challenges, love songs lament its loss, and those trying to function as singles complain—accurately—that the world is designed for couples. In short, even though coupling is a frequent source of our failure and pain, it is also the thing most highly valued by the majority of humans.

And for good reason. The emotional happiness and physical health of couples who succeed, not just in remaining together, but in achieving genuine satisfaction, are notably higher. Partnership success also has a favorable impact on our children and communities, whereas the costs of failing to achieve this, even when couples choose to stay together, are significant.

As a result of the value society places on successful partnerships and the benefits that accrue for all when we achieve this, a revolution for helping couples succeed is currently underway. Although it is a new revolution with few answers, numerous groups, including business and government, are joining the search for ways to attain stronger, more stable partnerships.

Yet in spite of this increasing and heightened valuing of successful relationships, we continue to have little understanding of how to attain them. In fact, this lack is so evident that while most couples on their way to the altar assume they will succeed and even boldly promise, "'til death do us part," statistically they collapse at about a 50 percent rate. What's more, the data for other romantic alliances that never make it to the altar suggest that even more relationships than those tracked by divorce statistics eventually break down. Other studies tell us that the stress levels of people enduring intact yet floundering relationships are so high that few would enter into such a venture if they knew these numbers or understood their impact.

There seems to be a disconnect here that demonstrates a significant level of cultural confusion. On the one hand, we place a high value on coupling. On the other, when people were asked in a recent survey which they would choose, a million dollars or their partners, half chose the money! So, while we have every intention of succeeding in our relationships, we enter into wedded bliss in a cultural context that is betting against us. And this bet is well-placed in spite of the value we place on our success. But how can that be? How do we value something so highly and still end up with such a poor outcome that we would put our money on it failing as we watch a couple take their vows?

How did this cultural voodoo, this stacking of the relationship deck and loading of the dice, become so mainstream, so acceptable? And is this low expectation for success the cause of relationship problems or the result?

We are not arguing that our culture's pessimism about relationships single-handedly causes relationships to fail. That would be putting the cause-and-effect cart before the horse. But it does appear that such a low cultural expectation for success, coupled with our culturally sanctioned inattention to our partnerships, work together to produce so many of these predictable disasters.

Can it be that simple? Can it be that raising the bar on our expectations for success and then paying more attention to how to reach this new standard is all that is needed? A closer look might help us to understand why it might be easier than we think to fix such a big problem with a few key adjustments.

A Closer Look at Relationship Failure

People generally desire the comfort and security of a committed relationship, but ironically, it is that very comfort that poses one of the gravest threats to the long-term health of most partnerships. Let us explain.

During periods of courting, we are usually on our best behavior. However, once we pledge our vows to each other, most of us start the move from our exemplary "courting behavior" to postcourtship or "marital behavior," drawn from the bottom end of the continuum of conduct. In short, we gradually sink into our less public, more comfortable selves, almost like slipping into an old pair of slippers after arriving home for the evening.

Unfortunately, in the process of getting so comfortable, we allow our unguarded, previously hidden parts to surface and be seen. This switch is often both abrupt and shocking and causes our partners to wonder what they have signed up for. The further out of alignment our careful courting behaviors are with our relaxed marital ones, the more dramatic this change is for both our partners and ourselves.

This is epitomized by an affable man named Ed who arrived in our office for premarital counseling with his fiancée Val. They seemed to be a match made in heaven—until the day after their wedding. Overnight, Ed took off his courting clothes and sat with a beer in front of the TV whenever he wasn't on call as a pilot. Val could no longer find the charmer she had married; nor could she get his attention or feel his touch no matter how hard she tried or how often we warned him that his previously concealed "Archie Bunker" persona would not hold Val's interest. Other couples have reported similarly swift changes in their partners, ranging from converting to a shrew while walking down the aisle to becoming violent on the drive home from the reception. Most fall into less extreme categories, with partners waiting at least a month or two before assuming "emperor status" or "barking rights." Regardless of what destructive new behaviors are adopted, they include things previously hidden and less attractive than the courting behaviors used to win the hearts of their partners.

The bottom line is that some time over the course of a few months to a few years following their commitment, most people slip from their highest, most appealing behaviors used to attract their partner down to the very lowest behaviors in their repertoire and points in between.

The question we ask is, Why? Why would anyone who wants to be loved by the person they have selected to share their life switch from attractive to repellent behaviors once they have won their heart? Why would they want to treat the person they love in this way or risk having that person no longer love them?

Why would anyone switch to harsh tones, clipped communications, and dropping out of conversations, where they were once careful, kind and attentive? Why, after hearing that their partners don't like this, would they slide even further down the scale? Why would people resort to impatient interruptions, short tempers, quick judgments, contentious arguments, or disdain and denials, where they were once enchanted, impressed and excited about learning from each other and exploring life together with ease and honesty?

Of even greater importance: why would anyone think their partner would remain enchanted and feel close to them when they insist on behaving this way? Why would someone assume their partner would be excited about remaining in such a relationship or want to continue to plan a life with them? And why would they conclude that after treating their partner this way, their own love for that partner would remain intact and continue to fill them with the happiness they originally felt in their presence?

Although these newly adopted behaviors are highly destructive to good feelings between partners, this is what the majority of people do in their interactions with each other once their courtship has ended. This ending is usually activated by wedding vows or some other form of commitment, though it may take some time following the ceremony to fully shift.

Typically it is the man who begins this cycle, causing the woman he so ardently courted with his interest, engagement, honoring and fullness of interaction to now feel unattractive, abandoned, lonely and, frankly, tricked into getting herself into a relationship that feels so utterly discounting, isolating and empty.

This in turn causes her to coach, then coax, and should these fail, to re-state her grievances or if needed resort to full pitched anger. If nothing works, she will adapt to her sadness and the pain of her losses and will then seek ways to live her life separately. During this period, she may also begin to obsess about how angry she is with her partner, possibly even plotting the details of her escape. Then over time, her plans for leaving no longer evoke sadness or anger, but offer her relief and the return of hope—hope that someone else will adore and attend to her.

Although men are often seen as the ones to initiate the distancing, which, in turn, provokes their wives to respond protectively, the reverse is also surprisingly common. Whoever starts it, the question remains: why would a couple move into their first home together, decorate it as tastefully as they can, and then move their worst personalities into the living room to relate to each other with a shocking lack of honoring and kindness?

Hanging On To "Who We Are"

The reason we persist in these unattractive behaviors, even when they are not working, lies in a confused sense of who we are. We each have our ways of being, our "who-I-ams" that we carry around with us and present to others. In this regard we have developed a rather reliable though static repertoire of interpersonal skills that we use on an unconscious, almost rote basis. Over time these skills become so automatic that we accept them as unchangeable and immovable and buy into the notion that they represent "who I am."

The problem is that many of our who-I-ams were formed during our interactions with parents when we were children. As a result, they reflect the same lack of maturity and impulse control that characterizes a toddler or teen, and are often filled with unattractive foot-stomping, temper fits, and days of pouting. These were also the behaviors we tended to persist in using, even when parents and others tried to talk us out of them. And because of this learned persistence, we continue to ignore the feedback we get from others when they try to tell us these behaviors are not working.

Another problem with these parts of ourselves wending their way into our personalities during our formative years is that the more familiar and comfortable we are with someone, the more we are tempted to abandon our better behaved public selves and revert to these more basic and comfortable, though childish and demanding, at-home selves. Consequently our less mature and self-centered who-I-ams become even more unguarded the closer we get to someone. And it is because of this closeness that we feel free to move these lower aspects of ourselves back into our lives and living rooms following our marriage vows.

The more out of alignment the charming self we put forward during courtship is from the less pleasant who-I-ams we revert to, the less chance our relationship has of working. Moreover, the more determined we are to use these automatic behaviors so readily available from our emotionally-charged, childhood repertoire—even after being told they aren't working—the more this persistent part of ourselves threatens our adult relationships.

Because this is what surfaces so quickly and automatically whenever we feel emotional or defensive, anytime something goes wrong in our relationships, rather than challenge these unworkable parts of ourselves, we revert to our less mature who-I-ams and then lower both barrels and fire away. If challenged by our partner for doing this, we launch deeper into a defensive posture or suggest that our partner is the one who needs to change. After all, this way of being, these things that I do because I've always done them is who-I-am. And I certainly can't change who-I-am.

The Preciousness of Our Partner's Life

The question we fail to ask at this juncture is, why? Why can't we change? After all, we changed our behaviors for the duration of our courtship, and we usually change a large portion of them when we are in public. Although these who-I-ams are the least attractive traits in our repertoire, we tend to save them for those we love most—the partners we have selected to share their precious lives with us. Yet by letting these who-I-ams stomp around and be in charge in our private lives, we fail to honor our partner or acknowledge that their life is as valuable as our own; and so rather than treat them with the respect they deserve, we feel free to treat them worse than we treat everyone else!

Not surprisingly, this failure to raise the bar on our post-courtship behaviors, coupled with our expectation that love will die anyway, keep our relationships careless and unkind, and thus unfulfilled and in danger of collapsing. Yet not only are we reckless, but unaware of the havoc we cause, for if we had any idea, we would stop. In fact we would stop as quickly as possible. If we understood how much our inattentive and dishonoring moments tear at the fabric of our relationship, we would behave in a diametrically different manner.

However, in our culture we are immune to the impact of these attitudes and behaviors, and so we feel free to act worse and worse. Then we wonder why our partner is backing away from us or hurting us in return. And over time, we wonder how the Velcro slipped and when we mysteriously "grew apart."

It is not part of our cultural consciousness to be aware of this treacherous dance that leads to our disconnection and breakdown. As a result, we don't train ourselves or others to stop acting out these less mature who-I-ams or learn to do something else. In fact, it is because of our pervasive lack of personal and cultural consciousness about this far-reaching problem that we unceasingly fail to address or fix it.

Current Approaches to Mopping Up Our Messes

As a result of the damage these low expectations of ourselves and our relationships create, it doesn't take long before the majority of us no longer feel as close or happy. Then in order to recapture the love we were so careless in protecting, we grasp at the idea that if we now enter into the therapy process, we will be able to identify and overcome the little devils, demons and trolls, the who-I-ams we have been indulging that are causing so much trouble.

And so, at this point couples enter into marital therapy in hope of learning to do things differently in order to convert predictable failure into predictable success. Therapists trained in a wide variety of methods eagerly join them in this therapeutic process, and off they go.

But has therapy been the answer to successful relationships? Divorce statistics that continue to hover around a 50 percent failure rate with half of the "survivors" still reporting unhappiness would suggest not. That is because the "helpers," including ourselves, have been focusing on the wrong part of the equation.

We have been tweaking the *visible* conduct we see people engaged in as a result of some internal belief they are holding about how to get what they want in life. And it is this internal state that is driving their external behaviors. But rather than help them adjust this cognitive belief in order to eliminate the emotional need for acting out the behaviors, we try to get them to stop the behaviors, thinking this will transform the relationship.

Although our results tell us that adjusting this end of the equation does not really work, we have not had better options to offer. But rather than acknowledge the futility of this approach or admit that we don't know what else to do, therapists usually suggest people negotiate the best deal they can arrange and then accommodate to their losses. And given the numbers, we can probably conclude that this is what a good portion of the 50 percent who didn't call it quits are doing.

This explains why so many people feel trapped in relationships that are not "bad-enough-to-leave," yet are on the edge of barely "good-enough-to-stay." They then feel empty, sad and confused about why they can't realize their most valued dreams of good partnership. Until now.

As a result of our strong desire to keep our own love alive, we started to dismantle the current myths about how to produce lasting relationships as an afterthought to so recklessly destroying them. We began to understand the importance of *frontloading* the process, rather than mopping up the messes after they were made. And so we developed a completely new approach that would allow us and others to attain far greater success at the outset and to start this process from the beginning of our commitment to each other. It would also offer those couples who want to recommit a genuinely fresh start.

A New Model That Opens the Way To Getting Beyond "Just Good Enough"

Rather than continue to use the old model that wasn't working for us or anybody else, we explored our own ideas about partnership. We examined our personal and cultural expectations, our combined therapeutic understanding of how relationships work, and our personal needs and ways of getting them met. In the process of re-examining the relationship process through this fresh filter, we created a new template that enabled us to identify those aspects of a relationship that we each required if we were to have it all.

To our surprise, a new, clearly articulated, no-nonsense roadmap for achieving the having-it-all goal surfaced. It was clearer than anything we had seen or used, and it seemed foolproof in helping us to resolve any issue that surfaced between us and to ultimately get us all that we wanted.

At first we used this roadmap solely for the sake of our own relationship. But then we saw that it offered a universal template that enabled participants in any relationship to quickly determine whether their alliances were ones that met their needs or in the more common vernacular were "working" for them. If not, they would immediately realize this and understand why.

Even more important, it provided a method by which such relationships might be corrected and expanded, with no limit on the possibilities for having it all. We started to work with other couples to share our discoveries, then small groups, and finally larger seminars. It was working for almost everyone and seemed helpful beyond our expectations.

Before long, we realized we were on to something big. So big, in fact, that it could be life-changing for individuals, families, businesses, schools, and friends. And it was even bigger than that. It dawned on us that our discovery was big enough to have a positive impact on our culture and times.

Once we grasped the enormity of what we had uncovered, we could see that our template had the potential to lift the lid of limitations from the human experience and free us to reach for unlimited possibilities along with our untapped potential for greater joy. We were in awe of our discovery and couldn't wait to share it with a broader audience. And so we decided to write *Settle for More!*

"The purpose of our lives is to give birth to the best that is within us." —MARIANNE WILLIAMSON

TWO

The Slippery Road to Barely-Good-Enough-to-Stay—But Not-Bad-Enough-to-Leave

"Here is Edward Bear,
coming downstairs now,
bump, bump, bump,
on the back of his head,
behind Christopher Robin.
It is, as far as he knows,
the only way of
coming downstairs
but sometimes he feels
that there really is
another way, if only
he could stop bumping for
a moment and think of it."

—THE WORLD OF POOH, A. A. MILNE

Whenever we ask in seminars or during counseling why couples act in ways following courtship that are guaranteed to destroy the love between them, most feel initially challenged to answer. But then as they further contemplate the question, it begins to dawn on them just how foolish a course

23

this is to take. Yet, amazingly, they still don't change; instead they persist in this startling shift in behavior that places their relationship in serious jeopardy. This is because we have all been culturally hypnotized by our group acceptance of this sloppy way of being in our primary partnerships. As a result, we have done it hypnotically and for so long that we don't easily wake up or adjust, even when we realize it is causing us to fall out of love and nudging our relationships into perilous trouble. So, once again the question is why? Why would we persist in acting in this manner, even after understanding how destructive it is to our highly valued partnerships?

Our Peculiar Urge to Do More of What's Not Working

A sensible friend of ours once suggested, "When you find yourself in a hole, stop digging." Good advice. And so simple to do. The problem is that most of us fail to heed this wise counsel and reach instead for bigger shovels. In fact, we have both noticed while working with couples in troubled relationships that what brings them to our clinical doorstep is their persistent use of an odd, yet popular, rule for living that goes something like this:

> *"If what you are doing is not working, try harder by doing more of it."*

As illogical as this sounds, it is shockingly common, especially when it comes to relationship problems. Unfortunately, this "doing more" response results in things like men talking less and withdrawing more, or striving harder to achieve dominance and control in the partnership. Women may then react by increasing their complaints or doing so in louder, shriller tones. These positions may also be reversed with many variations on the behaviors chosen. But the point is, if it wasn't working before, most of us will increase the intensity and do it even bigger, more often and with greater force.

However, much like Edward Bear—better known as Winnie the Pooh—while ramping up these dysfunctional behaviors in hopes they will eventually help our troubled relationships, we all know deep down that there really is another way that would be far more effective. The problem lies in our stubborn reluctance to abandon the behaviors we learned so well through years of practice, first with our parents and then with a series of partners. So again, the question is why? Why won't we extricate ourselves from a program that not only fails to get us what we want, but makes matters considerably worse? The answer lies in when and where we learned our individual ways of responding to the world and their importance to our personal identities, or "who-I-ams."

Although it's essential not to blame our parents or toilet training for the unkind behaviors we inflict on our partners, it is useful to understand that the lessons we learned as children tend to get woven either loosely or tightly into our adult relationships. Yet because the immature behaviors we learned while young are often not effective when we are grown, this early learning and the degree to which it gets intertwined in our adult relationships can become significant troublemakers, especially in our primary partnerships. Although we consider it pointless to spend time examining the *hows* and *whys* of the early learning process, we do consider it essential to understand the importance of letting go of those childhood lessons that are no longer working. The reluctance of most people to do this, while wanting their partners to do so, can best be described in the following dance metaphor.

How We Develop Our Personal Dance Styles and Who-I-Ams

Our personal dance lessons started early in life with our parents as our first dance masters. And we learned our lessons well ... in fact, so well that we accepted their steps as the only ones to use and claimed them as our personal who-I-ams. Unfortunately, because we were children with parents who were often confused about how to raise us, many of us inadvertently learned such things as being self-centered and stubborn.

Then when it came time to graduate into the larger world of interpersonal relationships we tended to use these same steps, even when the music had changed and they were no longer working. Only on occasion did we strive to improve our inter-actions with others by adding a new twist to an old move or perhaps an entirely new step to our repertoire. But for the most part, we persisted in using the same old routines, while at most dressing them in new clothes and occasionally donning a pair of fancy dance shoes.

So, if we learned early that being self-righteous and control-ling are useful tools for interacting with others, we include these in our repertoire and then search out a partner willing to trip the lights with us. On the other side, if our childhood dance coach gave kudos for such things as passivity or pouting, we seek adult mates able to counter-twirl accordingly. While initially concealing the worst aspects of what we learned as children, we strive to fill our dance cards with adult partners who seem to compliment our style. We then twirl left and they twirl right; we glide forward while they move back. Thus as our first dances begin, we move in a kind of unison with perfect cotillion etiquette while only occasionally stepping on each other's toes.

But over time as we relax into less conscious foot placement, the unexposed parts begin to bleed through and these more carelessly executed routines are no longer working. And so we dance harder, while telling our partner they aren't listening to the beat, have fallen out of step, or need to change their danc-ing pants. All the while, we are doing the only dance we know, the one we were trained to perform in our youth and the one for which we were so consistently rewarded.

Similarly, our partners, products of their own dance schools, are soft-shoeing to the best of their abilities, while scratching their heads and wondering why we have gone out of sync. We are each quite certain we are the one doing the correct steps. Nonetheless, one partner might offer some new variation to see if it improves things and, when it does not, reverts back to their more familiar routine with renewed vengeance. The other, feeling their partner's sequence is a tad rigid, while equally unwilling to alter their own, seeks a place of certainty found in the rote movements of earlier routines.

As the dance gets increasingly uncoordinated, with each partner evolving into a caricature of him or herself, they both become evermore convinced that the way they are doing it is the best method, if only their partner would understand and learn it. Then, not realizing the ridiculousness of it all, they ramp up their certitude and dance even faster and harder. The picture they present is of someone dancing so fast that their feet are a blur, all the while flailing away with the largest shovel they can find, going at breakneck speed deeper and deeper into the relationship hole.

If the discomfort gets bad enough, the partners, either on their own or with the help of a dance coach, attempt to improve things by learning to put up with the other's dance style or finding some new steps they can do together. While this may reduce the degree of toe-stepping, it does not get to the source of the difficulty and sets in place a rocky dance partnership and relationship of limited possibilities.

At this juncture, it begins to dawn on couples that they are in an arrangement that is barely good-enough-to-stay-in, yet not bad-enough-to-leave. They may even realize they are *settling for less* and sense a cloud of depression descending over their spirits. These are the couples we often see in our office confused about why they have "grown apart." More often than not, they both want to recapture the feelings that originally drew them together and get back on the dance floor with steps capable of returning them to the excitement they first felt with each other.

The Problem of Dancing with Lowered Bars and Outdated Steps

Unfortunately the dances we select following courtship are frequently drawn from the ones we used when we were young and immature and thus fail to support our adult relationships. From our point of view this shift seems like an easy slide into what feels so comfortable to us that we assume it will be as easy for our partners. Yet, from their point of view, the shift is both abrupt and jarring, and once these steps have been included, dancing together is no longer rewarding.

Although these behaviors may at times seem innocent enough to us, they are usually done with some level of awareness and are used in the service of getting our way. The more of these dance steps a person has learned during their early childhood and teen years, and the more they have practiced them in subsequent relationships, the harder it is to give them up. In fact, when we ask people why they persist in behaving this way, even when they know their partner is repelled by it, most simply describe it as comfortable. Unfortunately they feel relieved to be free of their more conscious yet formal courtship apparel and return to their familiar, though often self-focused and unappealing at-home selves—drawn from the less mature selves they learned from their parents during childhood and hate to leave behind. Not surprisingly, this switch is at the root of most partnership problems.

When asked why they would slip to this lower standard, many justify it by saying such things as, "I'm only human." This is a common phrase filled with the implication that humans can't expect much of themselves and have no choice but to live at this lower level of behavior learned during a period when they were self-centered and immature.

But, why? Why would we assume humans lack the capacity to go higher? Why would we view being human as a liability that compels us to be less, rather than an asset enabling us to be more? But even more important, why would we want an excuse for not growing up and being *more* or freely exploring the full extent of our personal possibilities?

Because neither of us has heard a good answer to these questions, we regularly ask people to reconsider how high humans might go and to challenge themselves and others to stop arguing for their lowest possible behaviors and to push instead against these self-imposed limits. Accomplishing this is well within our grasp and offers all of us a choice that is immeasurably more rewarding than failing to bother.

A Serious Problem

Living with partners reluctant to go beyond the immature lessons learned in early dance schools or to see any value in reaching higher can be both frustrating and limiting. Thus after a period of tolerable toe-stepping, the glue that once bonded such partners usually begins to give. These early rips in the fabric of their connection are invariably followed by larger tears, eventually causing the kind of deep scarring that can prevent this once waltzing couple from rebonding again.

When couples first notice that their love is waning, many reach for the rheostat switch that controls their feelings and begin the protective process of slowly withdrawing. Although this is done in the service of feeling safer, it is in fact dangerous to the survival of the relationship, since it initially leads to casual fantasies of escape and ultimately to more serious thoughts of divorce. Thus, much like the danger to relationship survival that a lowered bar and post-courtship changes in dance steps create, the rheostat switch serves as the third major threat to relationship survival.

To further add to their relationship demise, rather than find a way to communicate about the growing estrangement between them, most partners end up complaining to others outside the relationship or connecting with someone who better understands and values them. Yet these alliances, unless they are professional, can only serve to further separate the couple.

Each of these troublemakers work individually and together to produce the kinds of couples who feel caught in the tragedy of what we call "lump-along" relationships with no clear way to resolve them. Their quandry is due to so many early dance schools failing to teach them how to be clear, play fair or act as responsible and high level adults. This problem is intensified when one or both partners has attended schools filled with undue levels of unkindness, a general lack of clarity and a failure to teach that it's important to reach higher.

At this juncture, a somewhat serious problem presents itself. As a result of our culture's failure to provide realistic ways for couples in this predicament to right themselves, both parties derive a false sense of security from their lump-along arrangement and thus feel "comfortable" with their familiar, albeit unsatisfying, situation. This stands in sharp contrast to the fears they feel whenever they consider a change—and so, many elect to stay. Operating under the illusion that what we have in hand, even when it is not fulfilling, will be better than the unknown, both partners tend to cling to each other, even though they are, for the most part, unhappy. Our culture reinforces this tendency to hang on to unpleasant relationship security by honoring people who have avoided divorce and remained together for long periods of time, even at the cost of happiness, health, and in the extreme, life.

At the Crossroads of Settling for Less or Settling for More

It's clear that we have no cultural standard or method for expanding love or keeping it alive. In fact we measure partnership success by duration of time together, rather than the degree of satisfaction experienced. We have no happiness meter or guidelines for reaching a standard of excellence in our primary partnerships, even though having a good relationship is the human endeavor we claim to value most.

Because there is no cultural standard of excellence or a design for getting us there, most people fail to even try to create what we would consider a truly outrageous or out-of-the-ordinary relationship. Instead they simply react to whatever is presented, easily fall into unworkable patterns and surrender to lumping along in the limbo of alliances that are barely good-enough-to-stay-in but are not yet bad-enough-to-leave.

Sadly, couples who stay in these struggling relationships have *lowered the bar* on their dreams for a happy alliance and are simply trying to feel better in the context of their limited and limiting partnerships. Some will find this stifling. Others may feel it's as good as it's going to get. Yet the longer they persist in bumping along this pothole-ridden road, the less rewarding their relationship feels. Eventually, one or both gets tired of dancing with the other and looks around for new partners.

But then they remember how it was when they first met and felt so clearly in love. They may also focus on the needs of their children or feel guilty about breaking their marriage vows. Here, many will pause on the dance floor, take a second look at the other and wonder if there is yet another step they might try. It is at this point that many turn to therapy as a last resort.

So again, when we get down to what each of us most values and wants in our lives it is still the hope of finding and holding a primary partner in the context of a supportive, loving relationship. And it is this intense desire that makes us willing to learn some new dance steps—even if we don't like dance lessons. As a result, couples in trouble, often on the brink of divorce, go desperately in search of a wizard who might be able to help them.

Placing Our Lives in the Hands of the Wizard

That's what happened to Sheri and Jeff. They started with hearts pounding and stars in their eyes. Their souls were a perfect match, and each seemed to know what the other was thinking before any words were spoken. They also knew they would be life mates ... and beyond ... and were the couple pictured in most romantic songs.

Yet here they were in our office a few years later describing a relationship that was circling the drain. When we reflected their description of an alliance on its last legs and asked why they thought they could or should save it, Sheri defended the paradox by quickly asserting, "Because we love each other."

This couple, like so many we have counseled, was operating off the hope that love conquers all and thus assumed they were not truly at risk for soon being the owners of a past relationship. Yes, love does conquer all. But we don't really have a handle on who will be the conqueror or the conquered. For the surprising truth is, love has little to do with relationship survival. This is why we all know couples who are madly in love but are unable to make it as well as couples in relationships that look miserable, yet remain together for a lifetime.

What our dream couple was discovering was that we really stay in relationships for one reason and one reason only. And that is because the relationship in some way meets our needs. At first these needs include our higher-order needs to feel loved, honored and attended to. However, this may later be adjusted down to meet only our most basic needs for safety and security. This shift is made to accommodate our lowered bars and the subsequent changes this requires in our relationships, and many will even accept an illusion of security as part of this accommodation. By contrast, anytime a relationship meets all of our real and higher ordered needs and we are also in love, as Sheri and Jeff experienced when they first started, we have all the elements required for an outrageous relationship, one with unlimited possibilities. Yet, anytime one or both of these fall away, even though we elect to stay, our needs are no longer being met.

So what happened to this starry-eyed couple to cause a left turn as they were headed toward the life of their dreams? How did their relationship develop into what unfortunately seems to be the norm, rather than the ideal, as their happy beginning promised? Armed with all of the positive emotions and attributes of the optimal relationship, how did Sheri and Jeff get derailed and end up in the bin of lump-along relationships?

It is common knowledge that roughly 50 percent of all marriages wind up in divorce. But what is less commonly known is that among those that survive, at least half can be described as lump-along relationships, or those not-yet-bad-enough-to-leave but barely-good-enough-to-stay partnerships. And of the remaining 25 percent, a healthy portion will also slip into the lump-along category. In view of these numbers, what chance did Sheri and Jeff really have? Because they started with love and continue to feel some attraction to each other in spite of the damage and their full range of needs no longer being met, their wobbling results probably say more about the way we conduct primary partnerships in our culture than about them. The question is why. What is it in our culture that so completely fails so many couples?

The Importance of the Moment The Bar Gets Lowered

Most people's stories are remarkably similar to our ideal couple. And like them, we start with the promise of wonder, but then lower the bar on what we require of ourselves and our partners. This happens as a result of a cultural group-think that makes us relationship-stupid as we tacitly agree to this downgrade in our standard of behavior. It is also in this moment that things begin to become unraveled. When we ask people in our seminars to more carefully articulate why they would persist in using such destructive behavior, even after being told how much it alienates their partner, they sit stunned as they search within themselves for answers.

The consensus is that rather than strive for the best they can attain, most people go the other way at some point in their lives and succumb to their lowest standard of behavior. In primary partnerships this urge to let down seems to coincide with the moment it looks as though it might be easier for them to let things ride, to avoid issues, to "put up with" and to simply not address those aspects of their relationship that if not addressed will weaken its underpinnings.

While there are many benchmarks that lead to the deterioration of a relationship, the most critical and identifiable one is that moment when a couple actively avoids openly taking a stand on their expectations of their partner and themselves and, in so doing, lowers the bar on their standard of relationship behavior. As a result, their partnership is no longer operating on common ground in terms of what each can honestly accept, what truly makes them happy and how they genuinely want the relationship to be. Because there is no conversation at this point about how each truly wants to be valued and treated, there is no honest touchstone or point of reference they can return to and use as a guide for their interpersonal interactions.

This conversation is usually avoided because the first incidents that might naturally trigger it tend to happen during courtship or soon after a commitment has been made, and at this point in the relationship both are still actively trying to win the heart of the other. So, rather than have the conversation that would clarify their true standards for the relationship, one of two things may happen. The partner who normally gets pushy at this juncture may hide this tendency in him or herself. Or, if this trait bleeds through and gets exposed, the other partner, also wanting to be loved, may ignore it, rather than express his or her true concerns about such a controlling quality. Yet in this avoidance, the couple has lost an important opportunity to discuss how they will address some of the most critical components of their on-going relationship. Instead they have hidden the fact that there is a serious problem developing between them and fail to address how they each believe in handling things of this magnitude.

This avoidance and the lowered standard that accompanies it results in behaviors, emotions and reactions having no agreed-upon framework for genuine acceptance or ways to work them out. And without this consciously articulated and agreed-upon standard for the relationship, if one of the partners does not like the implications of some behavior, they are left with limited, usually reactive, options for dealing with it.

It is this early failure to create a true standard for their relationship that serves to slowly move the partners from a loving and kind, side-by-side partnership to one that places them across from one another, each seeking to be right, rather than responsibly honest. Once this oppositional position and the resulting battle are underway, their communications become personalized and defensive, or perhaps even combative, and lead to increased feelings of disharmony. This then becomes the setup for the adversarial nature of most of the interactions we see when couples first arrive in our office.

Typically, when relationships reach this stage, they are falling well below the line of acceptability and are close to being bad-enough-to-leave, or they have already reached that point and are going down for the count. Despite both partners doing more of what has not been working, they are unable to revive their relationship. They are now in desperate need of magic, agree to take a trip to Oz and are off to see the wizard ... or therapist. Once they arrive at the therapist's office, carting in their sinking relationship, they dump it on the floor and ask what they can do to fix it.

The problem at this point is that due to also being products of this shared cultural problem, very few therapists are actually able to help, and so the high failure rate for relationships persists. Chapter Three explains why our culture's current approach to helping does not in fact help.

"Have we exaggerated the barriers to our dreams?"
—DAVID HAYDEN

THREE

From Passion to Sticks: How Did We Get *Here* from *There?*

❧⚜❧

"Sticks and stones can break your bones ... and kill your relationship." —VARIATION ON AN OLD THEME

⚜

When couples like Sheri and Jeff get into trouble and seek help, their relationship history reveals the following picture. Like so many others, they started with passion, but somehow lost their way. Although every love story is different, original and with its own unique humanness, for most it goes something like this: Boy meets girl (or girl meets boy), and sometime after this initial introduction, one of them expresses an interest in the other and they have follow-up contact—coffee, water cooler conversations, an "accidental" run-in at the supermarket, lunch, a drink, something to connect them.

As the interest between them increases, so does the contact. Phone calls, email, movies, dinners, church, parties, concerts and weekend trips with differing levels of intimacy. During these early activities both tend to be on their best behavior. They are clean and perfumed, with manners and consideration for each other clearly in place. Animated conversations draw full attention and interesting responses, with flowers and cards punctuating the picture.

These are the courting activities that pull the new couple closer and bond their hearts with an invisible glue made of endorphins, pheromones, oxytocin, and other chemicals released by the body in response to feeling attracted, safe, loved, and attached. The power of these courting interactions and the connecting intimacy they engender are visually demonstrated in Diagram 1.

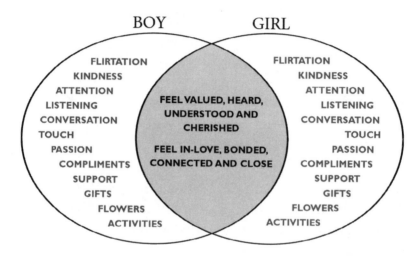

Diagram 1. Boy meets girl and *Courtship Behavior* begins, resulting in a strong bond and feelings of closeness, connection and being in love.

This diagram demonstrates how love can be intensified with the gallantry of courting, while nature responds to our positive efforts with its bonding chemicals to further cement our attachment and alliances. Yet interspersed with these positive and connecting activities are the various misunderstandings and unresolved problems that come between couples and serve as disconnecting dividers capable of dismantling the bonds they are forming and tearing apart the Velcro that attaches them.

These issues tend to arise after the couple begins to feel more familiar with each other and thus freer to relax the quality of their behavior. Unfortunately, it is also at this point of relaxation that the bar gets lowered and post-courtship behavior sets in. This slide into more careless interactions usually results in a series of upsets that, like sticks snagging on a fine silk fabric, create nicks and wounds in each other's hearts and a weakening in the fragile tapestry that bonds them.

These upsets or *sticks* are depicted in Diagram 2 cutting into their intimacy and breaking apart the bonds connecting the couple. Not only do these sticks interfere with the couple's positive feelings and closeness, they are capable of causing irreparable harm. Over time the nicks and wounds become larger tears, deep enough to leave scarring. The damage this causes to each partner's heart infringes on the strength of the bond between them and slowly eats away at their love for each other.

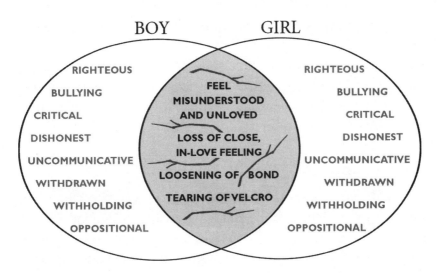

Diagram 2. After a commitment is made, *Post-Courtship Behavior* begins, resulting in a tearing apart of the good feelings, closeness and love.

Although we have assumed as a culture that the bonding chemistry felt so strongly between new couples naturally calms down sometime between six months and two years, this calming down is more likely a result of our lowering the bar on the way we treat each other and the sticks we allow to slash at the good feelings between us than it is about the calendar.

Since our courting behavior is what originally inspires our attraction to each other and when continued preserves it, we can conclude that if we would keep the bar raised and our post courtship behaviors at a considerably higher level, we would continue to feel bonded and passionate. The reverse is also true, and the tragedy is that so few seem aware of this obvious causal relationship between our stick behaviors and their effect on our feelings of love for each other.

Although there are a number of fortunate people who have somehow by-passed using the stick behavior and the twig piles it creates, Diagram 2 conservatively reflects the experience of eighty to ninety percent of the partnerships in our culture that have used it as their primary approach to partnership. Due to the impact of the sticks, once this most common, yet damaging pattern for relationships is set in motion, our initial feelings of love and connection are placed in a constant state of threat. Here's why.

The True Impact of the Sticks on Our Love

Most partners assume their sticks can be recklessly allowed to remain in the picture while snagging away at the good feelings between them. As a result, they feel free to speak in tense tones without kindness or manners, wage critical assaults on each other's personalities and engage in tiresome arguments and battles. In the process of doing this they slip into the habit of treating each other without the same care they would use with a stranger, much less someone who is loved and cherished. Clearly, this downgraded way of interacting causes both parties to feel embattled and betrayed, and the very thoughts about their partner that used to engender positive emotions now inspire disapproving ones.

Our culture supports the belief that these relationship-tearing behaviors, or sticks, should simply be tolerated as part of the partnership package and that even if they increase in frequency and intensity, the next level of stick turbulence should be accommodated as well. Yet by slipping so low in the way we think about and treat each other, we open the dark side of relationships which takes us in a destructive direction that will ultimately break down our good beginnings.

This breakdown is created by normalizing the expectation that love will slowly calm down anyway and that the battles will begin once a relationship is underway. We then laugh about the distancing this creates between partners and subtly support it with a number of cultural practices. These include such things as the assumption that following courtship, partners will no longer want to remain connected and are thus invited to return to many "singles" activities. Moreover, even when they are together in social settings the assumption is that they should be separated and expected to spend their time with others.

When these cultural concepts are taken to the next level, they include the notion that partners will also enjoy a little "harmless flirtation." In fact, a variety of business and social settings inadvertently offer opportunities for such relationship-busting behaviors. These concepts are further reinforced by such things as jokes that belittle marriage and mock spouses; songs that applaud affairs; movies that root for glamorous new paramours; and television shows such as "Everybody Loves Raymond" that denigrate relationships in general.

And so, with little conscious awareness on our part, there are many socially sanctioned attitudes and practices that create the stage for dishonoring our partners and playing with the kinds of sticks that can dangerously distance us from each other. Although much of this may take the form of good-natured humor, the chiding seems to support the underlying societal push toward having disconnected, and therefore limited and unhappy relationships.

As a result of this cultural mindset, when the sticks begin to fly and our twig piles start building, most of us fail to feel appropriate concern about the impact of the sticks on our love for each other or give them the respect they are owed for the danger they pose to our relationships. Thus rather than face the damage the sticks do to our feelings for our partners or their feelings for us, we join the popular trivialization of the process of falling out of love with our partners by making jokes about it.

And even though our break-ups include some of the most painful parts of our lives, we tend to insure the demise of our relationships by regularly viewing our partners through the latticework of the sticks, rather than the prism of the love and admiration we initially felt. In doing this we take our first steps to the dark side of relationships.

Once we have joined this dark cultural mindset and begin to act within its context, our attitudes and behaviors toward our partners often dip so low that if we truly thought about them, we would find them unconscionable. For example, we do such things as relax our criterion of behavior toward our partners the moment we cross the thresholds of our own homes each evening. Thus even when we have spent our day being courteous and caring to casual acquaintances we barely know on the other side of these doorways, at times exalting the roles they play in our lives, the moment we walk through the threshold of our own homes, we default to brief greetings, relaxed manners, negative thoughts, careless apparel and foul moods. We may even refuse to talk about our day and retreat instead, from those we claim to love most, into protective silence or culturally-sanctioned "caves."

In doing this we fail to cherish the person we have chosen to be our life partner or appropriately honor them for sharing their precious life with us. By holding our partners at a distance in this manner or forgetting to more deeply value their daily importance to us, we not only lose the opportunity for outrageous relationships, but slice away at the Velcro that once bonded us to the person we love and them to us.

In fact once we head down this dark, yet well-worn road, we are well on our way to a break-up, even if we remain together. Ironically, it is usually only after our partner tells us they have had enough of being dishonored and are ready to leave the partnership that we wake up and begin to view them freshly again. And it is at this point we stop perceiving them with the disdain that has become habitual and begin to view them again as others do, complete with the attractiveness we first felt for them. As a result, many want their partners back and return to courtship behaviors. But more often than not, by this time in the relationship, they are offering too little too late.

Their dilemma is exacerbated by the fact that most therapists working with couples whose relationships are at risk mirror the cultural mindset and thus tend to encourage partners to lower their bars as they rearrange and accommodate to their sticks. This results in continued partnership-threatening behaviors that, over time, shred the fabric and structure of our most important relationships. We suggest an entirely new approach, starting with eliminating the sticks.

Eliminating the Sticks

As destructive as they are, the sticks constitute a significant portion of most people's relationships. Yet once identified, they are simple to eliminate. The key is to just do it. But first you will need to know what it is you are eliminating.

In the section that follows, we identify the most common of the sticks that surface in our work with couples. While this list is extensive, it is by no means complete. We urge you to spend some time reviewing the list. See if there is anything in your current or past relationships we may have missed.

Most people are quick to identify the sticks their partner brings to the table. Unfortunately, this common reaction is normal and something you and your partner may have done before. In fact you have probably spent a great deal of time letting your partner know what he or she is doing or not doing that needs to change in order for the relationship to work. And your partner has probably reciprocated by giving you the benefit of his or her infinite wisdom regarding your flaws. This most likely has not been productive in the past and will be no more productive in the future. So perhaps this is the time to stop digging, rather than reach for a bigger shovel. If you want things to be different in your relationship, *you* be different. Here's how to begin.

Review the list thoroughly and honestly to uncover the unworkable behaviors and ways of being that you bring to the relationship table. Put a check mark next to those that apply. If you are appropriately relentless at this task, you will be surprised by the number of check marks you will generate. And that is the good news. You may now have some idea of what your contribution has been in your past and current relationships. So study the list in search of what applies to you. Be sure to be sincere in facing your part in things. Here's the list. Take your time. It will pay large dividends.

The Stick List:

Inattention to Creating a Positive, Dynamic, and Growing Relationship

- Fail to think positively about your partner or regularly focus on his or her admirable traits

- Fail to look at your partner freshly and anew, as though seeing him or her objectively for the first time as you do others and did with your partner when you were first falling in love
- Fail to greet your partner after time apart as if he or she is important to you, evokes positive feelings in you, and has your full attention
- Fail to think of ways to genuinely please your partner as you did when you first met with such things as careful listening, regular phone calls, emails, general caring, assuring touch, massages, a date idea, flowers, gifts, and helpfulness
- Fail to honor your partner as you did at first in such basic ways as dressing attractively, practicing courtship-quality hygiene, and using the manners your partner values and appreciates and that you use with others
- Actively withdraw increasing amounts of interest, time, touch, connections, conversation, caring, interest, and attention so generously offered during courtship, but then deny the truth of this if asked about it
- Fantasize about divorce, rather than address or fix the problems developing in your relationship
- Scan the field for your partner's replacement without giving him or her the courtesy of knowing you are no longer actively engaged in or committed to your relationship
- Fail to engage in such things as lingering gazes, extended touch, and longer, more meaningful kisses, as if afraid these may keep you from other things you now value more than a continuing connection with your partner; may lead to intimate moments you no longer value; or lead to a sexual encounter you no longer welcome
- Fail to comfort your partner when needed with such things as touch and conversation during "inconvenient" times or in the middle of the night as you did in the early stages of love

- Fail to suggest activities both partners might enjoy, such as dinners, movies, concerts, spectator and participation sports, shopping, travel, dancing and other ideas that would contribute to shared and bonding experiences
- Fail to respond enthusiastically to the ideas, activities, and suggestions of your partner but to put your heels down and refuse to try new things
- Subtly resist or outright refuse to give your partner the various things you know he or she enjoys
- Disparage conversation you once found enchanting and a means to more deeply understand your partner as now interruptive to the other things you would rather be doing
- Consider your partner's longer, more complex conversations as painful to endure, rather than opportunities for the mutual understanding and bonding they used to engender
- Stop valuing your partner or continuing to honor and pay attention to him or her, except when someone else is doing so
- Respond to others with the sparkle, eye-contact, enthusiasm and attention you no longer bother to give your partner
- Enthusiastically offer feedback, help and favors desired by others while avoiding offering the same to your partner
- Reluctantly respond to your partner's reasonable requests in a martyred manner, while "keeping score"
- Wait for your partner to do the things that will support your partnership before enthusiastically engaging in your own support of it
- Fail to notice or act on loving your partner in the specific categories and ways he or she prefers ... for example with verbal expressions of love, providing physical touch, offering favors, giving gifts, or sharing compliments
- Withdraw into the isolation of your personal "cave,"

whether through endless TV-watching, surfing the Internet or burying your head in the newspaper

- Return to the attitudes and activities of singles life following marriage
- Seek activities to do alone or with other friends while excluding your partner and rejecting ones he or she suggests or would also enjoy
- Withhold being honoring and nice
- Allow the original feelings of closeness, connection, and commitment to your partner to dim down during times when you are enjoying the company of others or feeling a bit superior, but then activate them during times when you feel less confident or not as involved with others
- Withhold compliments and other expressions of active love and support for your partner
- Refuse to let go and forgive even when your partner has sincerely acknowledged and apologized for their error

Overvaluing Yourself While Devaluing Your Partner

- Fail to view the partnership as a "we" and see it instead through the perspective of "me"
- Strive to meet only your own needs and get your way as often as you can manage it
- Seek superior status by puffing yourself up while putting your partner down
- Note your partner's foibles and errors with an attitude of disdain that suggests he or she is the only one subject to such weaknesses
- Elevate your own value, intelligence, skills, taste, contributions and opinion over that of your partner, whether in your own mind, directly to your partner or publicly to others

- Absorb the compliments and support of your partner in a way that causes you to feel superior to him or her while no longer acknowledging that your partner has comparable strengths
- Assume a position of superiority in the relationship in terms of good taste, good opinions and good ideas
- Set the bar of expected behaviors higher for your partner than for yourself
- Minimize your partner's contributions while exaggerating the effort and value of your own
- Use a disdainful tone of voice or body language that conveys the belief that your partner has less value, intelligence, validity and importance than you possess
- Constantly criticize, judge, deride and correct your partner and suggest ways he or she could be more like you or do things as you do them
- Ascribe negative attributes to your partner, often unfairly and unkindly developed, such as lazy, stubborn, self-centered, absent-minded, stupid, neurotic, foolish, oversensitive, pessimistic, a shrew, a jerk, negative, selfish, narcissistic, insecure, jealous, obsessive or spoiled
- View your partner as contrary, stubborn and unbending when they do not want to change the way they are doing something to the way you suggest
- Approach disagreements with the assumption that you are the only one who sees or remembers things correctly
- Regularly focus on your partner's liabilities in a way that results in your feeling less close and in love with him or her
- Fail to notice or acknowledge your partner's positive contributions to the atmosphere and feelings of your home
- Focus within your own mind on what is wrong with your partner, which results in a negative association to your partner and is thus a more dangerous pastime than is generally realized

Valuing Others More than Your Partner

- Enthusiastically value and highlight the attractiveness, talents, ideas and successes of others (including ex-partners) more than those of your partner

- Discount your partner's feelings and concerns while defending or taking the side of others (including ex-partners) who are ignoring, competing with or in some way failing to respect and honor your partner

- Give others (including ex-partners) the understanding and benefit of the doubt you do not give your partner

- Gently engage in conversations and even agree with others on topics for which you would take an opposing stance when talking with your partner

- Seek close connections with attractive people of the opposite sex by doing such things as telephoning and emailing them, setting up meetings and lunches or finding ways to work together

- Passively fail to notice the advances of others or establish appropriate boundaries with them by responding to their flirtations, holding their gaze when they extend eye-contact with you, allowing their touch to linger on you, or joining their lead in excluding your partner from conversation they are actively engaging in primarily or solely with you

- Listen and respond to others more attentively and enthusiastically than you listen to your partner

- Actively initiate flirtations with others and/or enter into extra-marital affairs

- Engage in sexual fantasies and idealized sexual associations with others—perhaps even during sex with your partner—an activity that renders you absent and competes with your focus and positive associations directed at your partner and will inevitably result in a loss of sexual interest in your partner and/or their loss of sexual interest in you

- Share intimate information about your partner when interacting with others, (including ex-partners), often done as a flirtation under the guise of discovering how you and your partner might solve your problems
- Seek intimate connections with others at a deeper level than the intimacy you create with your partner
- Ignore the discomfort your partner feels about other people making advances toward you

Winning A Presumed Competition with Your Partner

- Blame your partner for all that goes wrong while defending everything you do, even on those occasions when you realize you have made an error
- Claim "barking" or scolding rights
- Deny your part in communication breakdowns and other misunderstandings
- Adopt positional stances with the goal of being right, rather than seeking to expand your awareness, even when you know you are incorrect
- Behave in an oppositional, argumentative and righteous manner
- Resist everything your partner suggests and seek opportunities to disagree and fight
- Use a forceful voice and manner or even aggression to win disagreements
- Use passive aggressive behavior in order to cause hurt when you feel your partner has tried to boss or control you, or has won in some way
- Use passive aggressive behaviors to covertly express your frustration and anger, especially when you realize your upset

will probably not hold up logically if it is more directly and openly expressed

- Covertly complain about your partner to others when you do not feel you can get an equal footing in your relationship
- Freely engage in squabbles and spats without acknowledging the damage they do to the bond between you

Control

- Struggle over who is the boss by trying to control everything, whether it's the TV remote, the menu, or the checkbook
- Establish yourself as the one who makes the rules in your relationship, even if you have to employ anger, silence, pouting or passive-aggressive behavior to hold your position of dominance
- Control financial expenses to align with your own values and desires, while declaring that comparable things your partner values and desires are unaffordable
- Engage in passive-aggressive interactions in which you feign a desire to be fair and to cooperate, but then either very slowly, or never get around to doing so
- Covertly undermine your partner's relationships with the children, friends or business associates to assuage your feelings of envy and competitiveness
- Verbally attack or bully your partner
- Undermine your partner's confidence by withholding compliments, minimizing their strengths, ignoring their accomplishments, and dismissing their efforts to develop new ideas and talents
- Watchfully assess your partner's contributions to the partnership with an eye to whether or not they are doing their fair share while holding back your own spirit of generosity and fair participation

- Try to control the way your partner parents the children from their previous marriages, while insisting he or she parents yours with a different standard of fairness
- Be more kind and generous to your own children and grandchildren than you are to your partner's children and grandchildren
- Interrupt your partner's conversations with others to seize the spotlight, correct the details of their story or to tell the story yourself

Careless Communication

- Interrupt your partner and fail to listen to him or her with genuine interest, caring and compassion
- Fail to actively listen or truly engage, participate and respond during communication
- Divert your attention to other things such as TV or changing the subject when you disagree or are not interested in their topic
- Respond to your partner's communications with silence when you are not interested or disagree
- Listen silently during communication without engaging and thus take in the information without reflection and feedback or the opportunity for your partner to make corrections either to your perceptions or judgments about him or her or theirs about you

Negative Communication

- Withdraw, sulk or pout to demonstrate your unhappiness, rather than openly discuss your feelings
- Interrupt, debate, argue, oppose and resist your partner during communication

- Refuse to discuss certain topics you consider too uncomfortable for you to address and thereby block all opportunities to heal any partnership problems surrounding these subjects

- Obsessively revisit and express your anger about old topics previously discussed and accepted by both of you as having been resolved

- Covertly resist your partner by pretending to agree, then later act out disagreement in communication or action

- Dump anger on your partner when you don't like what they say

- Agree to disagree, rather than pursue conversations in greater depth in order to gain expanded perceptions and understanding in the service of finding a place of agreement or "the third story"

- Block the ability of your partner to get side-by-side with you during challenging communications by interrupting, using an unfriendly tone, and remaining combative

- Fail to provide enough uninterrupted air space for your partner to express the point they are attempting to make

- Debate and argue the validity of each piece of your partner's communication, rather than give them an opportunity to express their whole idea

- React negatively to your partner in response to a point you erroneously believe they are making, then hold onto that view and the associated negative feelings toward them, even after you have learned they were not making the point you originally assumed

- Listen with a sense of impatience, become easily agitated by what you hear, interrupt partial points made, jump to conclusions about the fragments heard, judge your partner for saying such things, then argue against these misperceived points without ever allowing your partner an opportunity to correct these misperceptions

- If your misperceptions are later corrected, acknowledge the corrections for the moment, but continue to perceive your partner through the original misperceptions and even return to quoting them during later disagreements

Dishonest Communication

- Fail to hold to honesty and integrity in your relationship with your partner
- Tell white lies to your partner
- Tell outright lies to your partner
- Keep secrets from your partner
- Fail to deeply and sincerely scan for and note or share the more subtle, elusive, nuanced, or shadowy truths felt within your own heart during sensitive or challenging communications
- Offer your partner quick apologies in order to avoid discussing in greater depth some error you have made
- Justify not sharing something with your partner in order to "protect" him or her from hurt or worry or the possibility of getting angry or distanced from you, rather than giving your partner the courtesy of knowing the truth and deciding how he or she wants to handle it
- Fail to admit your part in a misunderstanding, even when your partner has seen and noted it and has asked for acknowledgment and more opportunity for resolution
- Fail to truly acknowledge things you have thought or felt or done that are undermining to the relationship
- Lose interest in spending time, communicating, or being sexual with your partner without admitting the truth of this or giving him or her the opportunity to deal with the problem

Sharing Space

- Sully your shared space by making physical messes and/or sending negative energies into it without care or concern for the needs of your partner.
- Fail to understand that partnership includes sharing physical and emotional space in a way that lovingly honors your partner.

Although the entire bundle of these sticks is probably not included in the twig pile of your relationship, many of them have undoubtedly surfaced at one time or another, and the others can be found in the relationships of many of your friends.

Despite the commonality of these sticks, they are not as benign as you may assume and, in fact, are the primary obstacles to our relationship success. In truth, if our nervous systems were equipped to register the depth of pain these sticks inflict on our hearts or the degree of threat they pose to our bonds, we would wake up more quickly to their impact on our relationships and pull ourselves up short and stop playing with them ... even for brief moments.

For once a stick is used, it can be cleaned up but never fully recalled, since its effect is registered in our hearts as a part of our relationship history. This is why the notion of banking positive feelings and actions to counterbalance the debit created by the negative ones does not really work in relationships. Because the lens we use to see and feel things is shaped by all of our shared experiences, both good and bad, those experiences will all be included in the lens.

Now read the list of sticks again with the awareness that using even one of them at any time stands in the way of you having the relationship you desire. Ask yourself, "Why would I use any one of these with the person I love and have committed my life to?" Then ask yourself if the sticks are worth it and begin to think about what else you might put into your relationship beside the sticks. Next ask yourself if you are willing to stop using them altogether. Think again about what your relationship might look like if you remained in a courtship mindset and actively courted your partner for the rest of your life.

For those of you who assume this would be too difficult, remember that our periods of courtship are often remembered as some of the best of times in our lives. They are also the content of the movies we love most and the songs that move us. So why do we think that filling our own lives with the attitudes and behaviors of courtship would be "hard?"

This misguided attitude was once highlighted for Bobbie as she observed a kindergarten child lost in the joy of swirling her paintbrush into a glass of water where she could see the colors dance and play together in the spinning water. But when her teacher announced the end of playtime and the need to clean up, even though the child was doing the exact same activity in order to wash off her brushes, she switched her feelings from ones of joy to resistance and "suffering" as her shoulders slumped down and a pout swept across her face. Fortunately, Bobbie was able to help this child see that cleaning the brushes was not really "hard" as she had labeled it to be.

Similarly, lifelong courtship is not hard. In fact, it is easier and a good deal more fun for both parties than the postcourtship nonsense we have been trying to pawn off on our partners. It is fun to flirt and be flirted with by the person we love, to laugh and play, and to give and receive their adoration, attention and touch. It's what we miss the most after it has dropped out of our lives and what we then seek from others. So why stop?

It doesn't really make sense to do anything other than continue to be who you were when you first met, your best self, the one you knew you needed to present in order to win the heart of your true love. The question is why would we label this delightful behavior of our higher selves to be hard when in truth it is the sticks that are hard?

Why the Sticks are So Dangerous to Your Happiness!

Once we begin to understand the catastrophic effect the sticks have on the very fabric of our relationships, we can see that they represent the boogieman, the quintessential saboteur, the Fifth Horseman of the Apocalypse! And if they are not recognized as the troublemakers they are and dealt with immediately, they will make good on their job descriptions.

It is important that we understand this, for only then will we stop fussing with the sticks, complaining about them to our friends, or paying therapists to help us rearrange them. We must let ourselves see that the sticks masquerade as friends who will get us what we want, when in truth they are like cobras that stand between us and our happiness and must be dealt with accordingly.

For example, if you were able to get the attention of your parents by sulking or pouting, you probably still believe these behaviors will draw sympathy, love and attention to you. Although this may have worked when you were growing up, it is likely to push your partner away. And so, what was once your childhood friend is now the enemy of your adulthood.

Similarly, if we had families who picked up the messes we refused to handle or teachers who ignored the homework we failed to turn in, we may live as adults who believe our spouses will tolerate our lack of responsibility and happily do the things we resist. If our parents wanted us to win at all costs or made excuses for us when we wouldn't admit the truth, we probably learned it's okay to step on others' rights and then avoid taking responsibility for doing so.

However, we eventually realize most people aren't as keen on these behaviors as our parents or as tolerant of them as our teachers. As a result we learn to do them more covertly or master the art of passive resistance, in which we pretend to cooperate while doing something aggressive instead. These are the tactics that prove the most challenging of all the sticks for those who try to live with us.

So, review the list. Carefully absorb the definition and full impact of each stick. Is there any way you can imagine that these would be the tactics of choice if you were trying your best to get your partner to cherish, support, love, and want to be with you?

Bobbie once attended a seminar in which the leader suggested everyone who prefers short, serial alliances over committed relationships stand on the right side of the room. She then suggested that those who wanted to date these people go over and introduce themselves. Everyone laughed, but nobody moved towards them.

Our results would be similar if we suggested that those who like to dishonor their partners, conceal the truth, and look for opportunities to escape talking to them stand on one side of the room so that those who wanted to date them could find where they are. Now do this for each of the sticks on the list. You certainly would not write any of these qualities into your personal description for a *dating.com* service and expect your phone to start ringing. In fact you would probably make up a list filled with the opposite attributes. You begin to get the idea of how unattractive and destructive stick behavior really is.

So we ask again, why would you expect your partner to love and cherish and want to be with you when you use these tactics? After all, isn't that what you really want? To have your partner continue to love you, and for you to love your partner in return? If so, why would you do the very things that will guarantee you *not* to get what it is you want?

When we ask this question of couples working with us in therapy, the answers boil down to a blend of "I forget," "I can't help it," and "I think I will get away with it." Yet the irony of these answers is that in truth they *do* remember, they *can* help it, and they *never* get away with it! Moreover their failure to stop is the reason their partnerships are faltering and why they are in therapy. They are not getting what they want out of their relationships by using the sticks. Nor are they getting away with it. We never get away with it. Nor do we get what we want.

Using the sticks not only sours our partner's feelings for us but tends to trigger our counter-sticks in return. And once this back and forth "tit" for "tatting" is underway and the full array of our sticks are employed, it becomes a game that has no end. This expanding use of the sticks not only threatens the good feelings between us, but infects our homes to such a degree that both partners seek ways to escape the unpleasantness.

Because most people have assumed they really "can't help it," some will begin to realize at this juncture, particularly those in second and third marriages, that when they move, they will pack their sticks in the suitcases they take with them to use in their next relationships. Others realize with regret at this point that they are also leaving behind lost dreams, shattered families, and partners they once loved. They further realize that they lack the tools needed for creating better partnerships with the new people they have fantasized about meeting.

And so, at this critical crossroad sizable numbers of people become genuinely open to learning something new—hopefully in time to save their newly valued relationships and the families they have created. But to their great frustration, they discover that most of the "helpers" have no effective way to help.

Rearranging the Sticks

We all recognize ourselves and our partners in many of the unpleasant attitudes, beliefs, and behaviors we collectively call the *sticks*. Yet most of us assume these offensive behaviors are a normal, even acceptable, part of life. And so, rather than strive to be better, we have not only excused them, but put our efforts into adapting to their impact on our lives.

What we have failed to see is how dangerous the sticks are to our relationships as they slash across the bonds between us and cut away at the Velcro that connects us. Thus without much awareness on our part, they wield a powerfully negative impact on our feelings of closeness and mark the beginning of a breakdown in our primary partnerships. Yet, in spite of their poor record for success, the sticks described in the list are used regularly in some variation by most couples, and the more sticks we have, the more they threaten our relationships.

For example, Larry was too tired to talk to Ginny after work in spite of her pleading, but could manage to read, watch TV or even hit golf balls on his way home from the office. Then after years of loneliness, Ginny filed for divorce, and to everyone's surprise, Larry was both shocked and devastated. Although he thought nothing of using his sticks, even when Ginny complained, it never occurred to him that she was falling out of love with him.

Susie knew her angry scoldings were a source of great distress to Bill, but she argued that she couldn't help herself, and so she continued. By the time they came to us for help, on a 1-10 scale we use to measure the temperature of a relationship, Bill's love for Susie had dropped to a 2, while hers for him was still a 10. When Susie realized the true impact of her sticks, she was able to gain instant control over her scolding behavior.

The mystery to us is why people think they are so wonderful that their partners will want to stay with them, even though they are being unkind or add very little that is pleasant to the relationship. As Tom likes to put it, "Nobody is so good that they don't have to bring their best game to the party." And he gets puzzled over why so many people, particularly men, fail to realize this. We both wonder why anyone would want to live this way themselves, much less assume it would be fun for their partner.

It seems that many spouses enable their partners to indulge in using the sticks as a result of not keeping the bar on their expectations for appropriate behavior high enough. In fact many of these partners, often women, falsely train their partners to think their stick behavior is acceptable by failing to address it at the outset. Then after years of feeling unfulfilled in stick-filled relationships, these women finally act on their unspoken irritations and fantasies of escape. Statistics show that men trained by these partners to believe it's okay to indulge in their sticks are both surprised and devastated when they are left. When these roles between men and women are reversed, the results are the same.

So, you don't get to have the sticks for free. And the price you pay may be your relationship. Thus even if your partner is not letting you know that their love is fading or dying in the presence of so many sticks, there's a very good chance that is what's happening. As a result, when our stick count is still fairly low, and the bar to our expectations is also down, a relationship can limp along interminably. However, while we limp, the sticks continue to imperceptibly erode the good feelings between us. Though we might stay together, our possibilities for true happiness are seriously limited.

Stick Wizardry

Unfortunately, people are often slow to realize that their relationships are breaking down, and so they usually don't seek outside intervention until most of the damage has already been done. They will buy homes, cars and furniture in the pursuit of homefront happiness, but resist seeking quality help in achieving the best partnership available.

As a result, it often feels to us as if the couples finally seeking help have arrived in our office armed with several cans of pick-up sticks, with each stick well-polished from frequent use. They both dump their cans of sticks on the floor and then ask us to help them deal with each stick as well as the helter-skelter manner in which they overlap and interfere with each other. Once these sticks are on the floor it often feels as though we are supervising a playground full of children interrupting and squabbling among themselves with the singular goal of winning. And so even though their partnership is in serious trouble, rather than get out of the stick game that is destroying it, they usually focus on which one of them is right. As a result, rather than seek genuine healing, their therapeutic goal is to get us to adjudicate in their favor.

Most therapists get pulled into the role of judge and then listen to each story in an attempt to decide which partner is playing fair. Whenever a therapist falls into the role of judge, both parties attempt to defend their positions and sell the therapist on their rightness, rather than sincerely find ways to see and correct their part in the problem. As a result, their goal, even in the therapist's office, often continues to be some form of victory. To prevail, each partner may slant the truth to win the therapist over to his or her side. Yet in seeking to win these arguments, they not only threaten the love their partner feels for them, but are undermining the very process they are ostensibly using to pick up the sticks. If this continues, the outcome is predictable ... they will lose the relationship.

Depending on their personal point of view that is shaped from their own relationship history coupled with their training and temperament, different therapists will try to rearrange these piles of sticks in different ways. But even as they attempt to sort the sticks into some kind of order, one of the partners will invariably toss another bunch onto the heap. This is usually done in an attempt to gain the sympathy of the therapist or distract him or her from ruling against them.

An additional variable is that most therapists bring their own set of sticks to the table, including their personal values and biases. Thus a therapist with fuzzy standards may encourage one of the partners to continue dishonoring behaviors such as "innocent" flirtations or keeping secrets while learning to more covertly hide these dalliances. Another with a bias for couples staying together at all costs might encourage a victimized spouse to stay with an abusive partner, rather than leave and seek safety.

Better therapists may earnestly strive to arrange the mess of sticks into some logical order by encouraging the couple to do such things as "fight fair," "take turns talking," or "agree to disagree." Unfortunately these interventions often result in only short-term fixes that keep people together a while longer.

In truth it's rare that any of the therapists using these approaches get to the core of the couple's problem or achieve truly effective and enduring changes. As a result, statistics show that couples' counseling is rarely effective in transforming relationships and has not had much impact on the divorce rate or our failure to achieve happy primary partnerships. In some cases, the relief doesn't last for the week between sessions because the majority of couples have not only grown attached to their sticks, but to being right!

As you can imagine, a counseling office with one of these "happy" couples waiting on the sofa armed with their sticks can be a therapist's biggest challenge or worst nightmare, and many get as befuddled as their clients by the process. In fact it is well known in the profession that many therapists dislike couples' work, and a good number even refuse to include it in their practice.

We have personally been amazed by the pandemonium that has on occasion broken out in our offices in spite of our credentials and skills. One couple screamed at each other from the top of their lungs despite our threat to kick them out if they continued. At a certain point, it becomes clear that the available tools have been inadequate and that, *You really can't get there from here.*

Yet as grim as this can get, due to our culture's voyeuristic tendencies, watching couples in trouble has become a spectator sport on daytime TV, as their struggles expand beyond the privacy of counseling offices into the living rooms of millions of viewers. This new genre of "therapainment" is much like watching Judge Judy, mixed with the intrigue of an OJ Simpson trial. It is Reality TV at its most colorful—and pathetic—as charismatic therapists rise to the top of stick wizardry and then win America's heart by ruling against the most irritating of the partners in clever, humorous language.

The various Stick Wizards seem to rise and fall, and it appears their fixes are almost as temporary. The reason for this is that we can't get to the relationship we want through the stick pile. It's not that therapists haven't tried. In fact, it is pretty much *all* we have tried, ourselves included. But it simply doesn't work.

Is There a Better Way to Nurture the Love We Have Found?

The question is not who is the best stick wizard to referee which partner behaved the worst and must now be chastised into changing. The real question is why are we so careless with the love we have found and cherish? And what else can we use besides a lowered bar, post-courtship behaviors and the inevitable bundle of sticks to preserve and expand it?

When the two of us were fortunate enough to find love once again after running into each other, we made a decision. Rather than behave badly while trying to get the other to behave better, with or without the help of a therapist, we committed to finding something else … something completely different and new … something that would truly offer us and others the outrageous and joyful partnerships we all dream of having.

So strap on your helmets as we take you down this new and different road—a road that moves beyond the stifling limits currently set on relationships and leads you to new heights of unlimited possibilities.

"Laiz au lais bon temp roulette …"
(Let the good times roll.) —Cajun Party Cry

SECTION 2

Creating Our Dreams By *Being* All We Can *Be*

FOUR

A Better Way

"You don't have to plan to fail; all you have to do is fail to plan." —UNKNOWN

BOBBIE SAYS

Following our whirlwind courtship and commitment to being life partners, we had a few areas we needed to work out in our personal partnership. We could see the moment we hit these bumps how easily we could have fallen into stick-filled habits of careless communication and unresolved disputes, eventually leading to dishonoring each other and falling out of love.

We had both been a part of the stick-wizard cartel, with reputations for more success than many. Because of this we initially tried the same stick-fixing techniques with our own partnership that we had used with clients. But we could soon see that this approach was not going to preserve the kind of love we had experienced and wanted to continue. It had not worked in our prior relationships, and it was not going to work in this one.

Tommy was the first to realize we would have to find another road and engaged me in conversations to help us uncover what this might be. We spent hours talking about how to bypass the tendency to get into trouble at this stage of our relationship, and if it hadn't been for the challenge posed by our friends, we might have succumbed to the cultural tendency to passively allow our love to settle down as we slowly grew apart. But we didn't want to do this, and so we continued to seek new ways to achieve the kind of outrageous partnership we had both dreamed of having prior to reuniting and now wanted even more to continue after experiencing the depth of love we felt for each other.

The First Seeds of the Model

Soon after our search began, Tommy showed me a diagram he had drafted of a completely different model for relationships that revealed a new way we could relate to each other in a manner that would achieve our goal of truly expanded and joyful partnership. It was a simple picture depicting how we could bypass the pile of sticks we were starting to create between us and would have continued to build if we had not come up with this alternate idea.

He suggested that rather than continue to relate to each other through the lens that was getting increasingly tainted by the experiences of our slowly growing twig pile, that we reroute all of our thoughts and actions through a completely different channel depicted by a bubble he had placed above the sticks and labeled with a capital *"R"* to indicate the importance of the bubble as the container of our *Ideal Relationship*.

Next, he put two hearts along the path of the lines taking us to this bubble. The hearts had been inspired by a quality in me that I had learned while working with children and later with dolphins, both explained in the books I have written on those two very different subjects. This loving part of me resonated with his own good-heartedness, which became a more conscious component in his relationships after experiencing the steadiness of it in me.

Quite simply, according to this Diagram, everything we did to, with or for each other was directed away from the stick pile and done through an awareness of coming from our hearts and through the kind of relationship we dreamed of having.

This was to be the standard for the higher level *Relationship* he personally wanted to experience, knew I wanted, and wanted us to have. Under this model, anything we think, do or say must be consistent with the kind of relationship we desire and have identified as the one we want to be in; and as the model makes clear, anything that goes anywhere near the sticks is not consistent with this standard of relationship.

Now that we have both committed to this, it is startlingly apparent anytime our behaviors do not match our stated desires. And when that happens, it is not only jarring to both of us, but important that we notice the discrepancy between what we have said we want and what we are actually doing. It is even more appropriate for each of us to ask ourselves why we are doing something that is guaranteed to get us *what we do not want?*

As we both embraced the Model and practiced using it over the next few months, we expanded on the original concept to include *honoring* at the hub of our ideal relationship due to an inspiring experience Tommy had while serving as a consultant to an organization. The culmination of what we developed became our Model for Relationships as seen in Diagram 3 below. A comparison of this Model to the traditional stick relationship depicted in Diagram 2 and shown at the base of Diagram 3 graphically depicts the difference between the two.

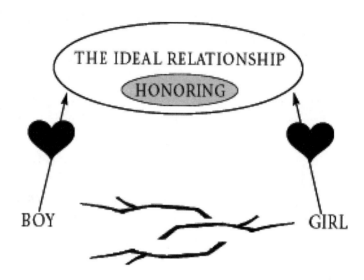

Diagram 3. Behaviors with our partners bypass traditional stick behaviors to insure they are consistent with the relationship we want to be in.

Honoring

Tommy's inspiring experience happened unexpectedly when he was invited to do a consulting job with a group of physicians. During the discovery period, one of the men expressed how honored he felt that his wife had pledged to spend her precious life with him. The doctor had fully grasped the enormity of this promise and subsequently spent their many years together honoring her daily while actively feeling grateful that she was in his life.

Perhaps it was because our love was so fresh at the time Tommy heard about this that the doctor's desire to honor his wife resonated so deeply within him. As a result of this timely encounter, Tommy committed to more consciously honor me in a similar manner for the rest of his life, a great honor in itself. I was deeply moved by this and offered him the same. This was so important to both of us that we included *honoring* in the bubble, and it became our primary partnership goal and first definition of the relationship we both want and want to be in.

As we were trying this on, Tommy declared that he would no longer relate to me in any way without first considering if it was channeled through this bubble and was consistent with his desire to honor me and our relationship. He added that by evaluating everything he did through the criterion of whether or not it was consistent with treasuring our partnership in the manner he had declared he wanted it to *be,* he would be able to determine if the way he was *being* or what he was *doing* was appropriate. I could see from his behavior that he had sincerely embraced this idea and was acting on it. I did the same with the same results.

We both realized from this that as long as we channeled *all* of our thoughts, feelings and actions related to our relationship through this bubble filled with our relationship goals and commitment to honoring our partnership that our behaviors would naturally reflect this honoring. And it worked. In fact it worked better, faster and more easily than either of us thought possible.

The surprising benefit is that the Model makes the standard for honoring behavior so clear that should either of our behaviors go even mildly outside of this standard, we are jarred into an awareness of being off track and immediately act to self-correct and right ourselves. A need for coaching and complaining is quickly eliminated as long as we are using the Model.

Once we started using the Model, it became clear to both of us that we couldn't go back and forth between the stick pile and this bubble that represented the kind of relationship we said we wanted and still have that relationship. If we truly wanted the open, loving, honoring, and seamlessly honest relationship we were jointly claiming to want, *all*—not some or most—but *all* of our behaviors would need to be consistent with what we had declared we want. It was also clear that our invisible behaviors would count as much as the visible ones. In addition, we had each become clear that we would hold to the standard we had adopted, regardless of what the other was doing or not doing ... and the Model helped us to see the raw truth of what we were doing and thus stay aligned with this agreement with ourselves.

And so it was during this typically shaky period following marriage when the sticks so often start to fly between couples as they begin to lean on each other for better behavior that we were embracing a completely new and wonderful way to interact.

Because I felt so honored, included, and trusting of Tommy as a result of the way the Model was helping him to select such high level attitudes and behaviors, I noticed my heart open even more to him as I fell evermore deeply in love. I realized that I was having a similar effect on him by my having made the same decision to conduct my relationship with him in this high-level, self-monitoring manner.

The bottom line is that the Model not only enabled me to more easily and clearly make decisions about how to act in our relationship, it helped me to stay aligned with who I wanted to be, regardless of Tommy's behavior choices. I was as excited about the Model as Tommy, and we both began to use it consistently. The result was that our love grew deeper and the joy of the relationship expanded exponentially. We were both surprised by the impact it was having on us and our partnership, and we started to share the ideas in our counseling work.

This was so successful we were invited to do seminars, and then a newspaper column. The feedback was phenomenal ... filled with reports of rapid, thorough change. One professional reported, "Once you get this idea in your mind, you can't get it out, and everything changes for the good." So how is it we get people from the sticks to the bubble so quickly? The secret is in the apples.

It's All in the Apples

One day while I was working with Lilly and George, a couple I had previously counseled for a period of time without benefit of the Model, I felt puzzled and a bit impatient that George was continuing to have so much trouble understanding the value of honesty in his life and in their partnership. I was grateful I now had the Model to help me explain it. And so I drew a diagram of it to clarify for George how his behavior had not taken into consideration the *we* of their partnership, nor had it honored his partner. But then I noticed the black bowl of wooden apples painted in burgundy tones sitting on the coffee table of my counseling room. I picked up one of the apples and said, "If this apple represents your desire to be an honest person in your relationship, which you have told me you want, you can't have the apple in your bowl some of the time and then pull it out when you decide to hide a lunch you just had with an attractive co-worker. Nor can you pull it out to cover up an email correspondence or phone call … or even the smaller things you know might irritate or hurt Lilly or reveal more of your true feelings than you want to expose. If you wish to be in an open, honest relationship, you can't yo-yo your *honesty* apple in and out of your bowl, nor can you take big or even the tiniest of bites out of it. The apple simply has to stay there, and then you can measure each of your behaviors against it."

Next I shared some of the apples Tommy and I had put into our *Relationship* bowl, such as *honoring, kindness, integrity, understanding* and a form of *seamless* and *open honesty* that knows no bounds. As I shared these, I went back to the diagram of the

Model I was drawing, turned the bubble into a bowl and filled it with renderings of apples. I then labeled these apples in accordance with the ones Tommy and I had chosen.

I then suggested Lilly and George do the same and instructed them to get very specific about what values and dreams they saw making up their ideal relationship. I added that since the apples will represent the construction of their relationship in the way they both want it, that it would be important to include everything they deeply value and care about and are genuinely willing to live by on a daily basis for the rest of their lives. They began the process of identifying their partnership goals and articulating their apples until the bowl was full.

Measuring the Appropriateness of Our Behaviors Against the Apples

After drawing renderings of the apples into the bowl, the Model became even clearer to me and easier to work with for myself and my clients. They helped me to visualize even more clearly that once we have defined the apples we want in our bowl, their visual presence helps us to decide which of our behaviors match our apples and are appropriate.

Once this is established, anytime our behaviors are not consistent with the values represented by our apples or the kind of relationship we have said we want, it becomes acutely apparent that we are temporarily removing one of our apples in service of some other, contradictory goal. For example, if I hold back discussing something I think might upset Tommy, I am removing the *seamless communication, open honesty* and *integrity* apples in service of my effort not to hurt Tommy" or to keep the peace. Yet in doing this I am serving the goal of *keeping the peace* and *not hurting Tommy,* even though neither of these are included in the goals—or apples—we have placed in our bowl. Although Tommy and I do value keeping the peace and not hurting each other, we also value accomplishing this with kind, side-by-side communication, rather than by sacrificing our apples.

As a result of the Model, and the bowl of apples to help us visually work with it, it becomes quickly and clearly apparent that avoiding these kinds of conversations is not consistent with what we have agreed that we want. Thus if Tommy becomes irritated or angry as a result of my sharing one of these communications, it is now he who has removed the *honoring, open communication,* and *understanding* apples in service of wanting to defend himself or be right, neither of which he has declared as a personal goal or a goal for our partnership. And the error now rests on his shoulders until it becomes uncomfortable enough for him that he puts his apples back in the bowl.

As a result of this bowl of apples in my life, it is easier than it has ever been for me to realize both the appropriateness and inappropriateness of various attitudes, thoughts and behaviors including the most subtle, nuanced thoughts carried in the privacy of my mind. It has also served as a clarifying guide to help me determine whether or not something I am thinking or considering is honoring to Tommy. For example, if I spend even a moment thinking negative thoughts about him in response to an impression I have that he has failed to fully listen or care about me, then I am not honoring Tommy as he deserves to be honored. And because we have raised the bar on the behavior we expect of ourselves and have included the *honoring* apple in our bowl, these negative thoughts immediately jar me awake to an awareness that I am not staying consistent with my goals and will thus fail to have the relationship I want. And so I immediately stop indulging in the dishonoring thoughts and return to ones that honor him, even if I am still feeling hurt. In doing this, it becomes quickly clear to me that I need to also remember my *honesty* apple and not only search my heart for the full truth of the situation, including my own contribution, but to then bring the topic out into the open and share with him any hurt that remains. When I do this with the honoring and gentleness that reflect the various apples we have selected, it invites a friendly conversation. Moreover since Tommy can trust that the *kindness, honoring* and *caring* apples are also in the bowl, we are able to talk civilly about this and rather quickly clear it up.

Once we begin to conduct our relationship this way, it feels generally wonderful most of the time. And when it does not, it becomes startlingly clear that one or more of our apples have gone missing. This can happen when one or both of us is not openly sharing something we realize should be shared. The withhold is *felt* both by the person doing it as well as the other. It infects our internal thoughts and feelings and becomes a blip on our relationship screen. And until this issue gets brought up and exposed, it will interfere with the unique clarity and subsequent closeness we usually feel in each other's presence.

And so once we have raised the bar and declared the apples we want to live by, anything, even if it is a little withhold, that we think or do that removes an apple is felt loudly by both of us. These wonderful results keep us honest and actively self-monitoring, since we both love and want to protect the way it feels when our apples are in the bowl.

As I began to tell other clients about this concept, I could see how easily the apples not only helped them resolve current problems but to also make progress on old issues that had previously remained immovable. For example, Tina had been scolding Jeff privately and roasting him publicly for years. They had come to me off and on to work on this, but the results were minimal, and Tina just wouldn't stop demeaning Jeff. Consequently, I was as surprised as anyone when, after agreeing to put the *honoring* apple in her bowl, she was finally able to stop all behaviors that were out of alignment with her stated goal. Once she declared who she truly wanted to *be,* any behavior that was inconsistent with her desire grabbed her attention and let her know she had slipped out of alignment with who she was committed to being. She confessed later that she was truly surprised to realize how often her thoughts about Jeff had been negative.

Similarly the *kindness* apple shocked another client, Barry, into a new level of awareness of his controlling behavior with Carol. And *deep understanding* apples promoted a new level of attention, focus, and listening in many of the men who didn't think they could do it prior to using the apple metaphor.

I was surprised by how easy the apples made it for people to see the inconsistency of their behavior with their stated goals for good partnership and how quickly they could now stop the things that were undermining their success. Of even greater importance, more of these people began to tattle on themselves when they had removed an apple because they were starting to see that removing the apples was spoiling the good feelings they were enjoying when all the apples were in. They seemed to grasp that removing an apple had also removed this quality in their own personal lives, and they wanted it back. The goal was no longer to get away with removing apples, but to stay aligned with them in thought and deed—since they had come to understand that this really was the key to their own happiness in the same way it had been the key to such happy times during courtship.

Carrying the Apples with You

Following our initial success, Tommy came home excited about another discovery. He realized that he liked to imagine carrying his bowl of apples with him wherever he went and to maintain his awareness of the importance of honoring the elements of the outrageous partnership we had designed at all times, even when we were not together. He later decided to apply the concept in all of his relationships. I realized the apples had also become equally important to me and of great value in assessing the appropriateness of *all* of my attitudes, thoughts, and behaviors in all situations.

Next, we considered how our relationship bowls might extend to include wonderful relationships with our children, grandchildren, friends and colleagues. It served as a clarifying Model for identifying appropriateness in all of our relationships and as such not only enhanced our primary partnership, but was expanding into all parts of our lives.

Then it occurred to Tommy one day that the way he relates to others and the world either honors or dishonors me as his wife, and this awareness further clarified for him his desire to be an honoring person in all situations. After hearing him describe this, I elevated my level of honoring him in all aspects of my life as well. As a result, neither one of us disdains the other to friends, responds to "harmless" flirtations, or talks disrespectfully about the foibles of the other's gender.

Over time we both refined this to include staying conscious of the most subtle, nuanced feelings and thoughts we carried in our hearts and heads and to keep these equally consistent with our apples. As a result of using this Model we were both becoming more and more aligned with our highest dreams for our highest selves. We were *being* consistent with who we declared we wanted to *be*.

The Power of Holding Our Apples

Once we both started to use this Model, we felt even more deeply loved, safe and loving. We wanted to give more to the other, not less. The gifts of attention, love, kindness and caring coming our way were so abundant that our biggest challenge was to find time for all the gifts we were inspired to give and receive.

This sounds amazingly simple. And it is. In fact, when the couples we have worked with grasp the fundamentals and tie them to their commitment to making it work, they have experienced a transformation in their relationships. And we have had the identical experience in our relationship. We are experiencing a constant expansion of our connection, love, commitment and most of all, joy in our partnership.

The only glitches come whenever one or both of us briefly removes an apple or two. And whenever we do, our relationship feels bumpy and jarring and clearly out of alignment with what we have declared we want. Yet because we are both using the Model as our guide, we almost always notice when we are the one who has removed an apple and feel anxious to return it as soon as possible.

Anytime this doesn't happen, there is a "feeling" within one or both of us that we are not as close, connected or joyful. Something is out of sync and we can feel it. But because of the Model and our experience that we are so much happier with all of our apples in the bowl, it doesn't take long before we want to fix it. In fact, we notice and correct it quickly, usually within a few minutes. Moreover, the conversation we eventually have about the bumpiness that has set in is guided by our understanding of the importance of noticing which apples are missing and to return them so that we may feel in alignment with our partnership goals again.

As long as we keep all of our apples in the bowl, our relationship remains outrageous, unlimited, and expanding. It's that simple. We invite you to have the same experience, and now that you have the Model, you can.

"What matters in the end ... is not the methods but the attitude behind them. If that is right, the methods work. If the attitude is wrong, the methods are meaningless."
—*P.W. MARTIN*

FIVE

The Power of *Being* Who We Truly Want to *Be*

*"Man is but the product of his thoughts;
what he thinks, he becomes."* —MAHATMA GANDHI

Once we understood that our goal was to raise the bar on our post courtship behavior and replace our stick behavior with carefully selected apples, we assumed the rest would be easy. But there was one more hurdle to clear. To get to where we eventually got, we had to take on the mantel of each apple. We had to *be* the apple. Let us explain.

Getting There

At first blush it might look like an easy transition from sticks to apples, simply because the sticks look so dreadful and the apples so appealing. Yet, as with other relationship models designed to help couples, it could end up being another goal unmet due to boring homework that nobody wants to do, forgetting the steps, or losing interest. But we have another way to guarantee your success with one simple understanding. So pay attention, because once you get it, you will never forget it, and relationship success is yours. Let us explain.

TOM SAYS

"You Can't Get There From Here" —Anonymous

While no one knows exactly who to credit for this common response to a directional query, mathematicians often use it in their conversations about proofs and formulas. We also heard it in reference to finding Pitcairn Island, but in that case it was with the caveat, "Actually you might be able to get there from here. It's just the slow way to do it."

Whether finding an answer to a math problem or the way to Treasure Island, the implication is that if you are too slow, where you are going may not be there by the time you arrive. And that is how we feel about the current approaches to relationship therapy. The methods used to help couples out of their messes—once they reach the point of truly wanting to change—are simply ineffective. As a result, couples rarely get back to treating each other the way they did during courtship. Thus, in spite of their attempt to return to the earlier feelings that the initial kindness between them engendered, few couples are able to make it back there by sorting out their stick pile.

In our attempt to help couples get back "there"—or to The Ideal *Relationship* shown in Diagram 3—before their partnership fails altogether, we offer a more direct route. So, rather than continue the endless and futile search for ways to soften, ameliorate, rearrange, or adjudicate the standard quagmire of relationship sticks seen in Diagram 2, we found a way to insure that *there* would still be around when they arrived. Here is how we did it.

New Ways of Getting "There"

The stick-ridden relationship in Diagram 2 is your relationship; it is our relationship; it is everybody's relationship at some point in our collective relationship histories. While it is a diagram of disaster, some manage to survive, though most do not. Thus, the failure statistic for relationships.

If relationship transformation is the goal, you simply cannot get *there* from *here* the old way—and *here* is represented by the latticework of twigs in your pile and the pick-up stick metaphor. So if at this critical juncture, you genuinely want to save your relationship, and you take your can of sticks to a therapist, dump them on the floor and ask for help in doing something different with one or all of them, at best you will be stuck indefinitely at the starting point while providing job security for your therapist. You will not be developing a relationship of unlimited possibilities. And here is the reason: You cannot get to the relationship you want by tweaking or rearranging the one you already have. Adjusting what we have does not fundamentally transform or alter our relationship.

It is similar to the futility of paying teachers more to teach our children and expecting better outcomes while changing neither the context within which they teach nor the content they are delivering. Increased pay for teachers using the same approach, perhaps with a few tweaks here and there, cannot improve your child's education. Things will still be the same, even if more books and computers are added. There will just be more of it. In short, more digging of the hole you are digging will result in a deeper hole. More or faster dancing with the steps you have been using will result in more of the same dance, done faster. But things will be the same at their core, and the outcome has no way of changing.

This is a multifaceted concept that, while appearing simple, is actually quite deep and requires some explanation. But once you understand and use the idea, it will dramatically change your primary relationship. In fact, it will open the door to new levels of effectiveness and joy in all your relationships, and thus your life and world.

Swimming Upstream Only Works for Salmon.

If we attempt to develop the relationship of our dreams by fine-tuning what we already do, we will be committing ourselves to a relationship life of swimming upstream. Fortunately, there is a better way to have the relationship we want, a relationship that is nurturing, safe, supportive, loving, seamless, and communicative. But most of us have been going at it the wrong way and consequently never get there. Here's why.

We meet the person of our dreams, decide that this is the one we want, get married, and then think we will now be in the relationship we have read about, seen in movies, or believe someone else has. We then settle into our dream of matrimonial bliss and do all the things we think will produce that state of being. But in spite of our efforts, available relationship statistics would argue that we are doing the wrong dance steps and digging a hole for ourselves. Somehow we got the wrong formula for getting what we want. Yet it is that same formula we keep using even when it's not working.

It seems that somewhere in our development as human beings, we adopted the notion that if we *have* what successful people have and *do* what successful people do, then we will be successful. And there are a lot of people making a good deal of money off of this faulty premise. Advertising agencies know it motivates a good deal of human behavior, and they play on it. This is why we buy the shoes that will lift us through the air, the lingerie filled with secrets of attraction, and the golf attire and equipment that adorns the winners. But there is only one Michael Jordan, few women have found Victoria's secret, and no weekend golfer equipped and outfitted in Swooshes is about to knock Tiger Woods out of the running. But we keep trying. Not because we are stupid, but because we have been sold on the idea that in order to be something or someone we must first *have* the right clothes, equipment, smell, hairstyle, car, awards, partner, bank balance, lessons, college education, and on and on. Even our kids spend much of their youth accumulating and then flaunting their attire, rather than delving within to uncover who's there. Once we have the stuff that successful folks have, we then assume we need only to *do* what they do, whatever that is, and we will be on our way to *there* wherever that is.

There is nothing wrong with wearing the most expensive basketball shoes, even if you can only muster up a six inch jump; spiffying up your body with sexy underwear if you don't mind looking like you are wearing someone else's garments; or being a dandily dressed and well equipped weekend hacker. Just do not expect that you will *be* anything other than that.

It's similar to the people on a spiritual quest who heard of a master becoming enlightened while eating an artichoke as he sat on a rock in the middle of a stream. Wanting to experience enlightenment, they decided to go in search of the rock, the stream, and the kind of artichoke he was eating. But it is not the artichoke ... nor the stream or rock. Having the paraphernalia will not get you to enlightenment, or anywhere else. You simply *cannot get to where you want from where you are.* You are going at it from the wrong direction. You are swimming upstream.

Changing Directions

To get out of this rut, we suggest that people begin to swim with, rather than against the current. This requires us to change a fundamental way we as a culture view how to attain what we want. A brief digression into the world of ballet and a story about Rudolph Nureyev told to me many years ago by a very special friend will help to clarify what I mean.

Those of us who have daughters are familiar with this scenario. Someone gets the idea that she should become a prima ballerina. (You can substitute sons for daughters and baseball's

MVP for prima ballerina.) Next we go out and buy a tutu and toe shoes, enroll her in lessons and launch her on her career. If we are lucky she will show an interest in the process for most of the summer. But at some point a toe shoe will go missing, she will need a new tutu, or she simply runs out of gas and her budding career comes to a slow, grinding halt, far short of the goal of *being* a prima ballerina.

We can see how this looks and why it happens in Diagram 4. We round up and *have* all the stuff and then get her to *do* what ballet dancers *do* by copying their actions, even if no fire has been lit within her. We cart our child to her lessons, watch her stand in the lines with the other children and struggle internally as she tries to push her body into poses and postures it wasn't meant to do. But then it dawns on us—and her—that this isn't quite what she had in mind when we talked about extra curricular activities. And we call it quits. Or if we hang in there a bit longer, she may land a slot as a lollipop in this year's Nutcracker Suite.

Diagram 4. Swimming Upstream
Having and *Doing* will not get you to *Being.*

Being Comes First.

Compare this to the story of Rudolph Nureyev, who reportedly arrived in Moscow from the Steppes of Russia for the first time at the age of twelve, saw the Bolshoi Ballet and was absolutely blown away. He was mesmerized from the instant the curtain rose and reported that *every fiber of his being responded to the art form, and he knew* at that moment that he *was* and would *be* a ballet dancer. He joined the Bolshoi at an age usually considered over the hill. Then with a focus shared by only the finest athletes on the planet, he *did* what was needed to rise to the premier position with the company in order to *have* the life he had envisioned and viscerally felt ignite within him.

Diagram 5 illustrates the difference in the direction of Nureyev's swim and perhaps more importantly, the outcome. Unlike our children, Nureyev did not start with getting or *having* all the appropriate accouterments, and then *doing* the work in order to *be* a dancer. He reversed the process and started with *being* a ballet dancer, feeling it deeply within every fiber of his soul. Only then was he compelled by the strength of his desire to *be* a dancer to *do* what ballet dancers do at a level that took him to the top. His perseverance and determination came out of the context of his early experience of *being* a dancer, which in turn allowed him to *have* what accrues to artists of his stature.

Diagram 5. The successful swim: First *Be*, then *Do* and you will *Have* that which you want.

The difference between Nureyev and our daughters is the direction taken in the swimming of the stream. He had to first *be* a ballet dancer, then *did* what ballet dancers *do* (practice, plies, bar work, diet, cross training, and so on) and then *had* what premier ballet dancers have. And this is the only way to get there. In fact, it's the only way to get anywhere.

The *Being* of Couples

When couples in trouble bring their stack of sticks to a therapist, they resemble the hopeful little ballerina *doing* all sorts of things in hopes that their efforts will transform their relationship into the one they want it to *be*. And so in concert with the therapist, they establish rules for their interactions with each other, learn the art of active listening, apply new formulas for taking vacations, more equitably assign household chores, establish financial fairness and on and on and on, etc., etc., etc.—*doing, doing, doing* whatever they feel will bring about the transformation they desire.

Yes, they are now able to fight fair, can make their partner believe they are listening, comfortably spend weeks away from each other, share in doing the dishes, squirrel away their money and feel empowered. But, the vast majority will not experience lasting change in the relationship, even though they have new clearer rules for living together. These forms of *doing,* while perhaps giving the partners some needed sense of order, connectedness, space, equality and/or control, are ineffective in producing long-term, change. This is because they do not address the fundamental problem, and so they cannot provide a template or road map to lead them to the relationship they desire. As the ballet example demonstrates, you cannot get there from where you are. Or as mathematicians often say, "You can't get there from here." You need to first change where you are. That is, you need to come from a different *here.*

The different *here* Bobbie and I ultimately established for ourselves is found in our *bowl of apples*. These *apples* represent the things we most value and want to have as the *substance* and *core* of our *Relationship*. The apples also represent the essence of the *more* we wanted when we decided to *settle for more*. As our *bowl of apples* developed, we realized it was filled with a collection of values that could be used as guidelines for all relationship success and thus serves as the true gift of this book. But to help you grasp the full power of this gift, we will offer a more complete explanation of how we discovered these apples that were harvested from a deep place within us.

WE SAY

How to Get to the *Here* That Will Allow You to Get to *There*.

For those older readers who are immediately thrown back into the earlier times of Woodstock, mantras and the era of "me" when they hear the words *being* or *beingness,* it is important to know that we are not using these words in the manner made popular in the 60s and 70s. Instead, we are referring to the strongly felt and thus more easily identifiable, multi-sensory experience of *being* one thing or another at some point in time.

For instance, if we were to ask you what it was like *being* in the most fearful (or wonderful) experience of your life, you would most likely be able to access that experience from your memory. But it would not be a simple one-dimensional snapshot. Research shows that significant memories are multi-sensory, and can actually be described in terms of all the cognitions and emotions involved, as well as the five senses: visual, auditory, tactile, gustatory and olfactory. Thus if you were able to recall the event in totality, you would be able to describe how the event *looked, sounded, felt, tasted and smelled.* You would also be able to round out your experiential description with the *feelings* and *attitudes* you had at the time of the event. In doing all of this, you would be describing how it was to *be* in the moment. And your description would be full-bodied and rich, with the texture of details mixed with your feelings and thoughts about the event.

Bobbie identifies this constellation of feelings and thoughts as the *energy field* in which the experience has been recorded by your emotions and mind and is then filed and stored within you as a full-bodied, multi-sensory "program." This program—or cluster of stored energy—is automatically called forth anytime something reminds you of the original experience or you consciously elect to remember it. Thus, if the original experience was strongly negative—as in the case of a life-threatening car or plane ride—you will feel uncomfortable anytime its *energy field* is activated by memories of it or even something similar to it. As a result of the way this works, you will tend to avoid things that stimulate this system.

On the other hand, if the original experience is highly positive, as in the case of a great adventure or personal victory, you will welcome all opportunities to revisit its energy field and the positive emotions this stirs in you.

In Rudolf Nureyev's case, his experience of the Bolshoi at age twelve was a strongly positive multi-sensory affair with full cognitive and emotional components. And it was out of the intensity and depth of that experience of *being* a dancer that his behaviors, or the *doing* that followed, took him to the top of his profession. He was where he needed to be in order to be inspired from within to get where he wanted to go. He was in the right *here* to get to *there*. Without this intense internal experience of *being* a dancer, he might well have only made it to a Nutcracker lollipop.

For couples wanting to settle for more, the right *here* is the *idealized dream* you most want to live in during the most intimate part of your lives—your time and experience with your primary partner. It is the *Relationship Bubble—or bowl of apples—* that you fill with your greatest, most valued dreams for the good life. And if you really get a multi-sensory sense of how wonderful it could *be,* you will be inspired from within to *do* what is needed to *have* it. And in the process, you will avoid the relationship equivalent of the Christmas ballet sucker.

So how do we do it? How do we get to the right *there—*or *being?* How do we start with the feelings that go with the end result? How do we get ourselves filled with the multi-sensory experience of it before actually having the experience? Read on, for we will now show you how to create your own Nureyev-like *Relationship* experience.

"Go confidently in the direction of your dreams and live the life you imagined." —HENRY DAVID THOREAU

SIX

Starting from the End to Create the Relationship of Our Dreams

※▷※

"To accomplish great things, we must dream as well as act." —ANATOLE FRANCE

⧓

BOBBIE SAYS

Ironically, both Tommy and I began to plant the seeds of *being* in this personal relationship we are now enjoying long before we realized it would be with each other.

Each of us had drawn from the strength of our intention to pull the relationship we wanted to us. While Tommy had done it as a result of being a person with naturally strong intention, I had purposely strengthened my intention by spending time during walks thinking—and feeling—what the end result would be like and imagining myself in the middle of the wonderful partnership I desired.

Wayne Dyer describes this process as a conscious decision to regularly *think from the end,* and in so doing to visually and viscerally *contemplate ourselves surrounded by the conditions of success* we wish to have. By setting aside time to consciously attend to this, we can generate the kind of internal conditions that Nureyev experienced and other superstars feel naturally, or consciously develop as I did. The value of having such strong feelings in connection with our goals is that they drive us to do what is needed to accomplish them.

Although the idea that we can participate in creating our dreams is deeply rooted in ancient teachings, including the Bible, there has always been a pervasive cultural reluctance to embrace this concept. As a result of this resistance, only the fortunate few who have understood and incorporated it into their lives have enjoyed the success that goes with it. Ironically, they have also become our cultural heroes and heroines who offer previews of what our human potential is.

For example many of our most famous athletes—such as Muhamed Ali, Michael Jordon, Tiger Woods, Andre Agassi, the Williams sisters and Lance Armstrong—are familiar with how this process works. And once they broke through to fame as a result of applying it to their lives, numerous others followed.

As a result of these athletes and others showing us the way, the idea of *being* that which we want is gradually becoming less and less alien or the unique province of rare people like Rudolph Nureyev and the other superstars who followed him. Today it has become believable, attractive and available to us all, and more and more people are beginning to claim and use it, including people like us.

In addition, science has recently begun to both recognize and explain how this works, which is freeing more and more people to tap into its power. In fact the scientific basis for this is summarized in books like *The Field* by Lynne McTaggart and the film, "What the Bleep Do We Know?" Both explain the theory behind why immersing in the *being* of an experience not only serves as the prelude to that experience as it did for Nureyev and later for us, but actually helps to draw the desired experience to us.

This is exactly what Rudolph Nureyev did naturally and without effort. And because he was aware of the feelings within himself, he was able to describe the intensity of his internal experience for us.

WE SAY

Fortunately, we have more than Nureyev's anecdotal account to support the validity of the power of feeling and experiencing the *being* of things prior to their expression in reality.

For example, sports psychologists have long used visualization to enhance the performance of athletes; in fact, studies have shown that visualization can be as effective as actual practice in improving athletes' performance. Because of such studies, we better understand that the Michael Jordans of the world do not appear simply as a function of practicing their athletic moves over and over and over and over again. They must first *be* players, filled with a deep desire felt as a sensory experience accompanied by intense visualizations of what that means. Only after this is in place do they start the process of *doing* the behavior required to bring the visualized and felt desire into action. Finally, the glue that makes the *being* and *doing* so powerful is *commitment* to the process that further ignites the feelings of desire within the individual.

You Too Can Create the Relationship of Your Dreams

The only way to get the relationship you want is to literally create it. The good news is that as a culture we are finally beginning to understand and accept that more of us can accelerate the creation of this and other dreams by actively engaging in visualizing and feeling our way into them.

Again, this is not some new-age psycho-babble, but a straight-forward, no-nonsense statement of what you need to do to get whatever it is you want. In fact, rigorous empirical studies in a variety of fields support our understanding of this empowering concept and show us how to take the steps required to tap into this ability to create and manifest ourselves and our lives as we want them to be. Although not previously identified, this includes relationships.

This is why it's so important for us to understand that if we truly want loving partnership, that can only happen by our *being* loving. And this is how we create whatever it is we want … by becoming the essence of whatever dream we hold in our hearts. This becoming starts with our ability to fully envision and *be* in it.

In fact, we believe that learning to create all the relationships you desire, starting with your primary partnership, is the first and most important step to learning how to live the life you want. And like any other goal, creating your ideal primary partnership begins with *being in your dream,* whatever that is for you. Here's how to uncover the essence of your partnership dream and then to create it.

Rebuilding Partnership Dreams

The first step for derailed couples to take is to honestly assess their current levels of desire and commitment to each other with the goal of finding a way to get their hearts back into it as vigorously as they were when they were first falling in love. Yet once the original bond is broken, it's not as easy as it was the first time around, and a very new and different road must be traveled in order to get back to *there.*

In order to begin this re-engaging process you must determine how badly you want your relationship to change, how much you want to continue with this particular partner, and how much you want a relationship of unlimited possibilities. If your desire for all three categories is intense enough it will serve as a spark that lights the fire of your visions and commitment. If only one of the partners is able to recommit, you can't get back to *there* because it requires that both parties jump all the way back into it and re-engage with genuine emotion sincerely and deeply felt.

In counseling and workshops we ask couples to do an assessment of their level of desire and commitment by asking the following questions:

- How would you rate your feelings of love for your partner when you first met, on a scale from one to ten?
- How would you rate them now?
- How high would you want this number to get?
- Do you believe you can get there?
- How would you rate the success of the relationship with your partner when you first met?
- How would you rate it now?
- How much do you want to improve your relationship with this particular partner, also on a scale from one to ten?
- How much hope do you have that this can be accomplished?
- How much would you want to have an outrageous relationship with this particular partner?
- How much faith do you have that this can happen?
- How do you think your partner would answer each of these questions?

We will assume that if you have read this far, you are in search of answers to these questions and would like to feel committed to making your relationship work—or perhaps even believe you might be ready to create the relationship of your dreams. Literally. While this next step is best done in concert with a partner you love, you can also do it on your own in preparation for creating the kind of relationship you want—as we did—so that when the right partner for you surfaces, you will know if they can pay the freight.

Whether you hope to find the partner of your dreams, rebuild an injured relationship or improve the partnership you are in, it is powerful to strengthen your feelings of *desire* for it to be all it can be. Here's how to do it.

Conceiving the Relationship of Your Dreams

You do not need to have literally dreamed of the relationship you would like. But if you truly want to get *there* from *here,* you are now going to have to visualize it with all of the senses you can muster.

Take a moment, preferably now and preferably with your eyes closed, to imagine that you have the relationship you always wanted, a relationship of unlimited possibilities. What would that relationship *be* like? In multi-sensory terms, what would it look, taste, feel, smell and sound like? In other words, allow yourself to create a multi-sensory experience of the relationship you would like to order up. Allow it to feel the same kind of intensity Nureyev felt when the curtain rose on the Bolshoi Ballet. As you develop this relationship experience, continually monitor any limits you are placing on your creation. Thoughts such as, "I really would like to have (fill in the blank) but I don't think that is possible," have no place in the creative process. You are developing your experience of a *relationship with unlimited possibilities,* one that is as good as you can possibly imagine. If you find yourself putting on the brakes, let go.

Now visualize *being* in it. Feel yourself there—*now*—rather than with a feeling of longing for it in the "possible" future, since this possible future is often accompanied by a fear that it probably won't happen or pain that it has not yet happened. You don't want the fear and pain of unfulfilled dreams to be the thing you are pulling toward you. So allow the spark, excitement and joy of your unlimited relationship to ignite within you in the present. Feel it *now*. What does it feel like to actually *be there—now?* Safe? Kind? Honest? Caring? Joyful? Vital? Playful? Supportive? Reliable? Synergistic? Understanding? Inclusive? Responsible? Honoring? Committed?

Next see yourself in a photograph that captures the essence of these qualities enveloping you as you are living in such a relationship. Notice the details and feel the feelings of the person in the photo engulfed in these qualities.

For some of you, either seeing or viscerally feeling this might be difficult. For others it may come very naturally and easily. And some can both see and feel it, while others easily feel it but can't see it. Or the reverse might be true. It doesn't matter. Any combination can work. The key is to visit this place visually and/or viscerally within yourself often and let it grow in your heart and expand into your reality.

Now you have within you the first sparks of the *beingness* of a relationship which will serve as the soil in which your particular relationship may grow. This is comparable to what Nureyev and other superstars experienced naturally, and the more often and intensely you consciously elect to experience it, the faster it will bring you results.

TOM SAYS

Visualize the Relationship, Rather Than the Person.

In doing this visualizing exercise with couples in therapy and workshops, we find that folks fall into one of two categories. When asked to describe their visualization experience, they will either describe the relationship in which they want to reside or the person with whom they want to have a relationship. You are going to want to focus on the former rather than the latter. Here's why.

The essence of the relationship is the framework within which you will be with a partner. That framework is what you want. Yes, you may want a specific person in the relationship with you, but creating the person you want first, is like trying to carry water without a container. The relationship is the container.

To understand this further, suppose you wanted to visualize the experience of a roller coaster ride. You would not only focus on the details of the roller coaster car—the seats, color, safety bar, size of the wheels, scuff marks on the paint, and so forth. You would focus on the clatter and clacking of the chain as it pulls the car to the top and then the rush as you hurtle straight down, gaining speed, weightless in the fall until you reach the bottom and almost immediately shoot back upward with the instant change in gravity pressing you into the seat and leaving your stomach at the bottom of the arch. Your experience might also include the food smells and sounds of the carnival and maybe even the flavor of the hot dogs or popcorn. The feeling state would be one of exhilaration, excitement, perhaps fear or euphoria. In other words, it would be an emotional, multi-sensory experience involving taste, smell, sound, sight and touch.

If you were to focus only on the car, you might be able to have a multi-sensory and emotional experience of your vehicle, even creating it down to the very last detail. But there it would sit. So, now you have the roller coaster car, but what about the ride? Without creating the ride, you run the risk of continuing to just sit there—or at the other end of the spectrum, of getting derailed as you swerve out of control around a particularly sharp corner. Without knowing what you want, you could end up on a ride with one unanticipated and potentially disastrous event after another, possibly leading to the demise of the ride. As a metaphor for relationships, the roller coaster ride can be wonderfully—and safely—instructive. For if you focus only on the person, you may be able to create the god or goddess of your dreams, your physical and emotional "soigner." You will then **have** *the person* you want, but this by no means guarantees that you will **be** in the *relationship* you desire.

This is why it is vital that you begin to imagine the relationship of your dreams. It's also important that you stick with the qualities you want in the partnership, rather than a composite of a person. And even if you have a person in mind, as Bobbie did when she put me on her wish list, be sure as she did to keep the elements of the relationship primary in your mind and heart. For if you have the person without the elements, you won't have the dream relationship. In fact, you might have created a nightmare relationship with a person you thought you could love who, unknown to you, lacks the very qualities or relationship skills you hoped he or she would possess.

When you start out in a relationship with a clear framework for how you want it to *be* already within you, it is easier to assess from that place whether the person joining you there is a match, or if they are in fact Mr. or Ms. Wrong. In order for you to stay aligned with the essence of the relationship you have designed for yourself, you will need to determine if the person you are considering fits.

Our Relationship Model and your own relationship structure work together to offer clear guidelines for assessing your compatibility with a potential partner. For example, do they want to be in the same sort of relationship you want? What does their idealized relationship look like? Do they share your standard of excellence? Are they committed to doing their part to achieve it? Do they actually demonstrate this in their attitudes and actions, or do they merely give lip service to it, but act differently? Have they ever thought about it before? And are they now willing to honestly discuss their desires and commitment for their ideal relationship with you?

These are all questions you should be asking if you want a relationship of unlimited possibilities, whether it's with a new partner or a partnership you hope to rebuild. If the person is attractive to you but does not share your dream, it can't work.

Thus it's important to face any conflict in this equation between the person and your ideal relationship as early as possible.

Upstream Partner Selection and Perseverance When It's Not Working

Creating the person first and then trying to develop the relationship of your dreams around that individual is another form of swimming upstream. Yet, it constitutes one of the most common partnership selection errors we make. It is the formula that causes people to think a relationship must be the right one because they love the other person. But love has nothing do with whether or not a relationship will work. That's an unexpected comment, so let me explain.

Holding the relationship we want in our hearts and our heads gives us the ability to discern between what feels good and what is right for us. Many times they will be the same, but when they are not, it helps to understand that we are hardwired in such a way that we will most often default to the one that feels good. It is the same wiring that keeps us in relationships that should have ended long ago.

But now we can use the Model, not just to help us assess if a partner truly fits into the relationship dream we have selected, but to recognize and face when it is time to override our hard-wiring and consider the option of moving on. By creating and holding our dream relationship in our hearts we can clear away the haze from our relationship-viewer and more clearly see if the relationship we are actually in is measuring up. If the person is not right, our idealized framework clarifies why the relationship we want cannot work with this particular person.

The Nuts and Bolts of Building the Dream

Now that you have the idea, and perhaps the multi-sensory experience of creating the relationship in which you want to be, the next step is to fill in the details and spaces. This step is analogous to designing a house. We can produce a rendering of how we might want our house to look, but that is only the start. To bring it into being, there are a number of things needed: structural plans that detail its innards, the selection of patterns, textures and colors, and how to bring it up to code. Here is where you get to fill in the blanks that will provide the substance for your particular relationship.

One way to begin this step is to ponder *who* it is we want sitting in our living room, eating at our dining table and sleeping in our bed and to then begin the process of putting that person into our lives, beginning with ourself. Note that we are not looking at our partner here, but ourselves. It is the person in the ideal picture we visualized earlier, a person filled with the personal qualities we value for ourselves and want in our lives.

Bobbie describes how she began the process of creating the relationship of her dreams by employing this concept in the following way.

BOBBIE SAYS

During the months before I bumped into Tommy, I spent at least a half hour each day writing down and then dreaming in a quasi-meditative state about the way it would feel to be safely tucked into a kind and loving, brightly conversant, supportive and joyful relationship in which I felt deeply understood and cherished by a partner actively interested in spending time with me. I simultaneously felt what it would be like for me to be deeply understanding and cherishing of my partner and actively wanting to spend time with him. I would then add images of myself cozily immersed in a deeply loving and bonded partnership, including such things as humor, adventure, laughter, and play, along with a unique level of seamlessness and open honesty, all anchored in a heart-filled connection with each other, nature and God. I picked these particular qualities because they are the ones I value most and wanted to be sure were abundantly filling my personal being and life.

I had started the ball rolling of being the first one to *be* the qualities I wanted to have in my living room and life. I started by putting them in my own heart and being so that I could take them with me wherever I went. And by having them tucked within me, they became the magnet needed to draw those qualities contained in another person to me. Without this step, I could not have attracted my current relationship to me.

WE SAY

Begin the *Being*

At some level we all want a primary partner who so deeply loves and cherishes us that he or she consistently treats us with honoring, love and kindness. Yet most of us fail to act consistently with honoring kindness and love in our personal lives. We do so briefly during the period when we are performing our courting rituals and dance in order to be seen as attractive. But once successful, we usually abandon this more willing and attractive approach to loving partnership and replace it with an interactive pattern of waiting for someone else to begin the process of being consistently loving before we are motivated to respond in kind. It seems we falsely assume that once they get the ball rolling, it will be safer and easier for us to follow suit.

Yet by waiting for someone else to start the loving, kind, and honoring behaviors before we are willing to surrender our less attractive who-I-ams, we by-pass our own, precious opportunity to be loving and kind people contributing to peace in our relationships, homes and parenthetically, the world.

Also, in the process of looking for others to get things started, we often get impatient and angry about their delays and then feel justified in bringing forth our very worst selves in the service of monitoring and scolding them. This causes additional friction and fighting, which drives us further from *being* the person we want to be or from realizing the wonderful relationship we say we want.

So, rather than continue on this outdated path that so consistently fails to produce the intimate, supportive, and loving partnerships we have been hoping for, we must be willing to get out of the starter's gate and be the one to begin the process of *being* loving and peaceful in a real manner from deep within ourselves.

This is an odd, almost topsy turvey concept that fails to make sense to us until we try it. But once underway, the magic of how this works takes over, and for the first time we are able to understand it! So give it a try. See if you can be the first off the blocks to bring love and peace to yourself, your home, your life and your world.

Select Who It Is You Want to Be

Now that you understand the Model and how to use it, it's time for you to develop exactly who it is you want to be and what it is you want in your particular apple bowl. To do this, you will want to go back to the ideal relationship you saw in your visualization when you imagined it being the best it could be. Keep in mind the values you most cherish and want to be sure are a part of your life and partnership. Then incorporate all of these components into the apples you select to represent who you want to be and the relationship you want to be immersed in on a daily basis for the rest of your life.

We will give you a start by sharing in detail the ones we have selected and why. This is one of the most important steps you will take into a wonderful partnership and life. So off to the orchard to select your apples!

"Go confidently in the direction of your dreams and live the life you imagined."—HENRY DAVID THOREAU

SEVEN

The Apple Bowl

*"We are each others harvest; we are each others
business; we are each others magnitude and bond."*
—GWENDOLYN BROOKS

Interestingly, when we review the things we most value, the
majority of people put their primary relationship at the top of the list,
along with God and their children. Yet the time, attention and energy
they invest in this valued endeavor is inevitably given their lowest priority. The irony of this is that if you don't put any time or thought into
what you want in your relationship, your chances of getting it are a
crapshoot at best.

Would you be willing to enter into a truly life-changing
event with no more than a 50 percent chance that it will succeed? Because, if you are married, or contemplating marriage,
that is exactly what you are doing. We have discussed these statistics earlier, but they are worth repeating: one out of two first
marriages end in divorce. We refer to this as the one-out-of-
two-statistic—or ooots—a term we will be referring to throughout. Second marriages are no better ... two-out-of-three—or
toots. And third marriages? One study found that over 90 percent of these don't go the distance.

Given this reality, if you decide to attend to your relationship, rather than continue to ignore it, the first step will be to more carefully uncover what it is you want. That may sound obvious. However, we find that when we ask couples if they know what kind of a relationship they want to have, they uniformly say "yes." But when asked to describe in more detail what it would look like, they seem to have trouble articulating their vision. They will provide a general sense of it, as if they are hitting the highlights of what most people would consider the "ideal" and then possibly add in some idiosyncratic twists to an otherwise uncreative wish list.

And so we suggest that you take some time to more deeply consider exactly what kind of partnership you would like without setting any limits whatsoever on your dream. Make it as grand as you can possibly imagine. And if you find yourself restricting the dream in any way, let it go.

As you create, envision and develop your relationship in this more careful detail, begin to pay attention to the words you are using to describe the experience. What are these descriptors? Write them down as they begin to take shape, for these are the definers, the words you will use to clearly articulate the relationship you want to *be* in.

You will want to develop your list independent of others, including your partner if you are currently in a relationship. These are your descriptors of what you want. While they might be the same as your partner's, they might not be. You don't want to be influenced by what others assume constitutes the ideal relationship nor do you want to feel you need the agreement of anyone else for your personal creation of your dream relationship.

The goal will be to live by whatever picture you develop on a daily, moment-to-moment basis. So take the time needed to make sure it is truly what you want.

TOM SAYS

It's All in the Apples ●

The metaphor Bobbie described earlier and has used in working with individuals and couples in therapy and that we now use in our work together is one of a bowl of apples. We suggest you use the same metaphor. Visualize a big bowl, and as you identify one of the things you want in your relationship, think of it as represented by a gorgeous red apple and place it in the bowl.

You may be wondering what kind of thing would go in the bowl and feel unsure of where to begin. We have spent a great deal of time refining our bowl of apples, and while they may not be the same as those you will come up with, hearing about our apples will give you a better idea of what we are talking about and the importance of fully defining each apple.

The way we went about it was to ask each other, "What kind of relationship do you want to *be* in? If you were to be in a relationship of unlimited possibilities what would it *be* like?" I answered with: I would like to be in an ● **Honoring relationship**, one that is ● **Committed,** ● **Honest,** ● **Spiritual,** ● **Loving,** ● **Intimate,** ● **Connected,** ● **Inclusive,** ● **Safe,** ● **Sexual**, a relationship with ● **Seamless Communication,** ● **Humor,** ● **Integrity**, one that is ● **Expansive** and ● **Passionate**.

These identifiers were not included casually. Because by stating openly that they were the apples being placed in my relationship bowl, I was saying that anything I did to or with Bobbie would have to be consistent with my apples and the relationship in which I wished to be. To do anything else would mean, by definition, I would not *be* in or *have* the relationship I wanted. In fact, the apples became the touchstone for my behavior, the guiding principles by which I would have to run my life if I was to have the relationship I wanted.

It is that simple: First get very clear about the kind of relationship in which you want to *be*. Identify the hallmarks of your vision, the apples if you will. Second, make sure everything you *do* to or with your partner is consistent with your apples, and that by *doing* so, you will always be *doing* what is needed to *have* the relationship you desire.

But be aware that the obverse is also true. If what you are doing is *inconsistent* with what you say you want in a relationship, you will not be in or have the relationship you say you want.

Here is something else to consider. Simply identifying the *words* to describe your ideal relationship and then following the cultural norm of using careless, post-courtship relationship behaviors is not going to cut it. Guaranteed. If your behaviors fail to match the apples you have claimed to be your standard, your partner will just go away, and you may not know why. You will need to do the things that will continue to win his or her heart. So begin by asking yourself what this would include.

The following list gives you a look at what we mean. The definitions have developed over several years and we are very comfortable with them. They are the lines we have drawn that shape our relationship and within which we operate with each other.

There is a caveat and disclosure here. Our apples are aspirational. They do have an idealistic quality because that is what we are striving for. Do we miss at times? You bet. The difference is that in past relationships if we felt something was missing, we really didn't know what it was. With the apples, we know full well whether they are in or out of the bowl, which gives us the ability to immediately do something about it. We don't have to go through the common everybody-loves-Raymond, Albee-esque harangue, trying to get our partner to do it "my way" because I am right. There is never, we repeat *never*, a need for that behavior because it simply is not consistent with our apples.

We have given you the Webster definitions of our apples followed by our own experiential definition starting with my take on them, then Bobbie's. Read them, think about them and imagine what it would be like if they formed the basis of *your* relationship. Here they are:

Tom's Apples

⬤**Honoring:** *implies profound respect usually colored by love, devotion, or awe; to show high regard or appreciation for.*

> *"I could not love thee, dear, so much*
> *Loved I not honor more."* —Richard Lovelace

For me, this is the big one ... the single word that most clearly states the way I want my relationships to be. I want them *all* to be honoring. Look at the definition. If you will sit with that definition for a while you will begin to see the enormity of it all. It sets the tone for all the apples.

In my relationship with Bobbie—one that starts with profound respect—the love, devotion, and awe that I feel provide the robust color and texture that make it singularly special and spectacular. It is exactly the relationship that I imagined and am fortunate enough to be in.

And if I want the relationship to continue, then I need to be honoring in my behaviors, or *my doing.* I need to honor Bobbie ... always. Not just during the week, or an hour a day, but always. Not just when we are out in public or when I want something from her, but always. Not just when she is around, but always. I don't flirt with other women or talk with the boys about "my ol' lady." That would not honor Bobbie or the relationship ...

it would not reflect the profound respect, love or awe that I have for her.

We have heard couples say, "You mean you have to be like that *all* of the time?" And we answer, "Yes. Why would you want to be any different with the person you love and with whom you want a relationship?" They will frequently respond that they do it "most of the time," and then describe their interactions with each other in a way that suggests they honor each other, at the most, 50 percent of the time. Now, 1 out of 2 will get you a .500 batting average in baseball. And with that batting average, you can negotiate million dollar contracts. But relationships are not a game. A .500 batting average in marriage will not get you the brass ring, a million dollars, or the key to the relationship of your dreams. At best it will get you a lump-along, and there is a high degree of probability it will bring about the end of the relationship you say you want.

Being honoring, having a profound respect for Bobbie, means I do not argue with her point of view, but try to understand it; I do not play take-away in an attempt to manipulate her to get what I want; I do not withdraw to the company of my exclusive friends. And it means that *all* the apples are in play, *all* of the time. Read on.

◑ **Honest:** *free from fraud or deception; of unquestioned authenticity.*

"Being entirely honest with oneself is a good exercise."
—Sigmund Freud

This one seems so obvious. Everybody says they want an honest relationship. No one says they want to be in a dishonest relationship. But you would never know it by observing their behaviors. From the simple response of "fine" when asked, "how do you feel," and you really don't, to denying having an affair when in fact you are. And we know that this latter little bit of dishonesty is closer to being the norm rather than the exception. Although there are many layers of dishonesty that would precede an affair, getting all the way to this outer limit of deception is surprisingly common.

In the course of the therapy we do with couples, we have heard stories of all shapes, sizes and colors about partners' infidelity to each other. Thinking we were quite familiar with the subject, we were floored when we began to look at the statistics. In fact, many years ago Geoff Hamilton, one of the best family law attorneys in the business, and I did a study of 300 divorcees. We developed a wonderful body of proprietary data. One of the surprising statistics was that roughly the same percentage of men and women (40 percent) reported having had extramarital affairs, which is similar to the numbers uncovered by Kinsey in his landmark study in the 1940s and 50s. He found that 50 percent of married males and 26 percent of married women had dallied in at least one sexual relationship by the time they were 40 years old.

So, now we come to the 21st century and find that honesty has not gained any ground. Quite the contrary. In fact we see a consistently upward trend in the numbers of both men and women reporting affairs, with the number of women diddling around outside of their primary relationship growing at a much faster rate than men. A conservative guestimate offered in the most recent research is that 80 percent of all marriages have at least one partner doing sexual exercises outside of the relationship. What is remarkable is that the writers cited this statistic, not only to urge the reader to accept the incidence of infidelity as reality, *but to accept it as the cultural and societal norm and deal with it as such.*

This is a terrific example of the cultural push to lower the bar on our expectations for relationships. It appears that the 80 percent factoid is within the ballpark, but I take exception to the call for acceptance. It flies in the face of my notion and Webster's definition of honesty.

Gregory Popcak in his book, *The Exceptional Seven Percent*, identifies 7 percent as the number of marriages which he considers exceptional. This correlates well with the figure we have pegged for those marriages/relationships that are outrageous, or unlimited in their possibilities. Popcak argues that relationships can be the vehicle to inter- and intrapersonal transformation and provides the "secrets of the world's happiest couples," who he feels have used the vehicle to do just that. However, no such state of relational euphoria can occur in the absence of honesty.

While I have focused most of my thoughts here on the issues attendant to infidelity, honesty is pan issue. It is one of those things that has an off-on switch. I can't be mostly honest, or honest some of the time, or honest in everything except some teeny area, and have it work.

As for me? I want an "exceptional" marriage. I want to be a part of the seven percent. Without honesty it will never happen. Take a look around. Do you see any exceptional, outrageous, unlimited relationships that are absent honesty? I do not. So, I am signing up to *be free from fraud or deception, to be of unquestioned authenticity.*

⬤ **Spiritual:** *of or relating to the moral feelings or states of the soul as distinguished from the external actions; reaching and affecting the spirit; influenced or controlled by the divine Spirit; having a nature in which a concern for the Spirit of God predominates; proceeding from or under the influence of the Holy Spirit; concerned with religious values; seeking earnestly to live in a right relation to God.*

I was raised in a loving home by parents with unassailable values and strong feelings of spirituality. It seemed natural, and I mimicked many of their beliefs, but never really owned them for myself. It was like getting the Cliff notes so I was able to pass the exam. But the problem came when I needed to draw on the material in my life, and I found that the depth of my knowing was not sufficient and thus of limited utility.

So, I spent much of my early adulthood trying to figure out what I should have learned, and certainly had the opportunity to learn, earlier in my life. Two marriages and several significant life changes later I got the message.

I have always felt incredibly lucky and blessed by the way things have continued to turn out, being certain that someone else has been driving the bus. I could not have received the remarkable gifts that have been given me by my own doing. I have always been very certain of that. But until about ten years ago it had been somewhat of an illusive, abstract and comfortable concept, one that barely reached conscious recognition and certainly did not require that I act on it.

Successful in my business, healthy and with wonderful friends, there was still an absence that was impossible for me to explain. Through a series of events which included a failed marriage, I was introduced to the notion that I could have a personal relationship with God. Knowing that up until that point I had not been particularly successful in my relationships with significant others, I was not all that confident of how I would do in one with the Creator. And it seemed a bit daunting.

Ten years later, I can't imagine being without my spiritual relationship. I am constantly made aware of the realness of the connection. While it is a work in progress for me and often a struggle with my part of the relationship, it is a firmly planted part of my life and my relationship with Bobbie.

We came to Christianity on different roads but turned up at the same place at the same time and firmly believe that our deceased parents and God gave us a nudge. We are also moderate in our practice of it, focus on the message of love and are careful not to press our version of spirituality on others, but strive instead to simply and gently live it. Yet we feel so strongly about our partnership with God that we have memorialized it in our corporation, Gibson Grace & Merrill. Gibson is Bobbie's maiden name, I am the Merrill in the equation, and Grace acknowledges our belief that the work we do is a function of God's grace. And for both of us Grace has been abundant.

Including the *Spiritual* apple is simply a given. I want all the wattage I can get in my relationship. The *Spiritual* apple enlarges the scope and robustness, giving us a purpose greater than ourselves and a sense of loving and being loved that up until this point in my life was unimaginable.

🍎 **Loving:** *to feel affection for; hold dear; cherish, to feel a lover's passion, devotion, or tenderness for; to cherish or foster with divine love and mercy; to feel reverent adoration for; to like or desire actively; be strongly attracted or attached to; delight in.*

The apples in my bowl are universally applicable. They define the kind of relationship I want to be in ... with everyone. Bobbie, my office manager, the bag checker at our local grocery, the wonderful man dancing between passing cars as he sells papers to their drivers, my intimate friends of whom I have a few, my not so intimate acquaintances of whom I have many ... all of them. And that goes for the *Loving* apple as well.

While I want to be in loving relationships with everyone, that doesn't mean that they are interchangeable. The kind of love in the relationship determines the form and content. Some, like my relationship with Bobbie, are paramount, singular in nature. Others are casual with little requirement. Robert Sternberg uses a model that I like to describe the different kinds of love.

He says that love is a function of three primary components, Commitment (C), Passion (P) and Intimacy (I). We can diagram a relationship as a triangle with each component forming a side of the triangle (Diagram 6.1).

Diagram 6.1

Sternberg posits that the nature of the love in a relationship can be determined by the shape of the triangle. For example, the kind of love a parent might have for a child would look like the triangle in diagram 6.2; long on commitment, less so on intimacy and even less on passion. While we are certainly passionate about our children, it's not the same type of passion one would experience in their primary or significant-other relationship.

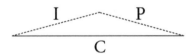

Diagram 6.2

And then there is the kind of love someone experiences when they say they fell in love in a bar with a total stranger, had a few drinks and went home with them (diagram 6.3); long on passion, zip on intimacy and commitment. The diagram is consistent with the relationship one might have when they say they are in lust.

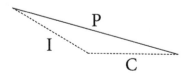

Diagram 6.3

You can see that just about any kind of relationship might be diagrammed using commitment, passion and intimacy in a way that we would be able to get the nature of the relationship just by viewing the diagram.

A couple of points here. Sternberg feels that the length of each side of the triangle and thus the shape of the triangle will change as a function of time. He says that passion is the first to enter, coming along at the outset, with commitment and intimacy building throughout the life of the relationship. He offers no opinion about the shape the triangle needs to be. Rather, he says that what is important is for both the partners' triangles to be similar in shape. This makes sense if you think of what a relationship might be like if the passion, intimacy and commitment of partners were significantly different in terms of degree.

So if you decide you want to include love and loving as apples in your bowl, it is important to articulate the kind of love you want for this particular relationship. This also requires that you come to grips with and have some understanding of how you want to include commitment, passion and intimacy in that relationship.

Me? My ideal is to have an isosceles triangle. I want full quantities of passion, commitment and intimacy and will take as large a triangle as I can get.

◯ **Committed:** *to obligate or bind to take some moral or intellectual position or course of action; to pledge to some particular course or use.*

> *"It is a trap for a man to dedicate something rashly*
> *and only later to consider his vows."* —Proverbs 20:25

Commitment is one of those things that when present significantly increases the odds of you getting what you want. Without it, you run the risk of being on the down side of the ooots.

So, from a practical point of view, I want the *Commitment* apple in my bowl ... always. By *obligating, binding* and *pledging* myself to my relationships, I have a vested interest in the outcome that simply is not there in the absence of commitment. I am making a statement about my intention of *permanence*. I have *ownership* of and a *responsibility* to making it work. When rough spots surface I don't get to point the finger at Bobbie, insisting that she take care of it ... because *I* am responsible for "it."

When committed, I am placing myself in a position that is more than a lip-service distinction. It is a no-nonsense, this-is-where-I-am, you-can-count-on-me ... 100 percent. Not 95 percent, but 100 percent ... *all of the time.*

Commitment is a big deal! A quote from Goethe reflects my feelings about my commitment to Bobbie and the magnitude of its importance:

> *"The sum which two married people owe to one another defies calculations. It is an infinite debt, which can only be discharged throughout all eternity."*

And that looks like something very different than the kind of "commitment" we are used to.

Again, the ooots tells us that half the people who commit to each other in marriage bail on their commitment. While certainly there are times when terminating a relationship is the best alternative, we know that the best results happen when both parties agree to the termination. However, no-fault divorce suggests that culturally we support folks unilaterally breaking their commitment to each other. I don't know how we decided that it was a good idea for two people to commit, to pledge and obligate themselves, and then let one decide they weren't going to do that anymore. It is a guaranteed set-up for failure. So you can see that this does set up a sort of conundrum. On the one hand, there are times when divorce is the appropriate alternative. However, it seems that it is increasingly the automatic default position when things aren't going well in a relationship. Being committed does not mean stay in it at the risk of physical or mental injury. On the other hand, bailing on your commitment because you're bored, have changed your mind, or whatever the reason du jour might be reflects a belief that commitments don't count. But they do count. For me, commitment means to give myself away. I learned early on in life that you can't give something away and then take it back. That is a fast way to become persona non grata on the planet. But we seem to be saying this is ok in relationships, which contributes in a big way to the looseness in relationships, the growing apart that we frequently hear about in therapy and is the antithesis of what we are after.

🌑 **Intimate:** *of or relating to an inner character or essential nature: innermost characteristic of the genuine core of something; marked by a very close physical, mental, or social association, connection, or contact; showing complete intermixture, compounding, fusion; thoroughly or closely interconnected, interrelated, interwoven; showing depth of detailed knowledge and understanding and broadness of information from or as if from long association, near contact, or thorough study and observation; marked by or as if by a warmly personal attitude especially developing through long or close association, by friendliness, unreserved communication, mutual appreciation and interest; manifesting warm personal interest; showing or fostering close personal interests and relations rather than those colder and more distant, formal, or routine.*

Intimacy is a word that frequently comes up in therapy with the couples we see, usually having to do with the male partner's inability/unwillingness to connect. When the topic of *intimacy* surfaces, the query arises, "What do you mean by intimacy?" Most everyone has some idea of what that word means to them, but when they try to articulate it, they have the same difficulty they would if they were trying to describe a feeling. Somehow, we don't have the words at our command that are necessary to communicate the robustness of what we feel.

Though rather long, Webster's definition above gets close to it for me. There is sense of depth, connection and vulnerability. It is the antithesis of shallowness and surface interaction. It is usually the thing that is absent in early courtships, in that it requires a willingness to expose oneself, warts and all. And that is the last thing that we normally would want to do.

In fact we present our best side and if we do a really good job, we get the person to like us, and if all goes well they love us. And now we have a lot at stake in NEVER opening up, because the person we got to love us doesn't know about what is inside. They may think they do, but it is only the material we feel safe to show, material that we feel fairly certain will be liked. It is this self-protection that severely limits our relationships

Look at the *intimacy* training we are exposed to as we wend our way through childhood into adolescence, then into young adulthood where the courting rituals are in full bloom. While there are gender differences in the way the hiding of ourselves is manifested, it is part of that ritual for both males and females.

Seems to me we train our males to be everything but open, honest and fully vulnerable about our emotional and affective side. Obviously, this is not just my good idea. People have long disagreed about what precisely is the source of the emotional restriction that we see in men … "mother blame," "boy biology," "testosterone," etc … though there is little disagreement with the fact that the restriction exists.

My thought is that as a culture we inadvertently place boys in emotional handcuffs from which many never become free. Dan Kindlon and Michael Thompson in their masterpiece,

Raising Cain, fully explore the roots of the emotional training we give our boys and the disastrous results of this "emotional miseducation." Young boys who do not learn to deal in a healthy, open way with those painful emotions that are a developmentally natural part of the socialization process, will suffer for it. Both the child who finds himself as the painful object of the bully, and the bully, are learning maladaptive methods to deal with their feelings.

The strutting, posturing and acting that boys do with other boys and girls, while giving them an artificial sense of comfort and belonging, is simply a culturally acceptable way of hiding. This training is insidious, all-pervasive and unrelenting. It launches our males into the world with a full set of emotional armor that is designed to allow them to move stealthily through the emotional mine fields of relationships unscathed. It also keeps them unconnected, unfulfilled, and empty. Ironically, we are guarding against the very thing that is needed if we are to experience the depth and fullness we all want in relationships.

So, how do the emotional little boys in the grown up bodies of men free themselves and become intimacy experts? First, we need to understand that we simply have to if we want to be in successful relationships. This is the place for the leap of faith, because we need to trust that it is the way to get what we want when our history has trained us to believe the opposite. It is a process that requires a safe relationship, one that will support our emotional growth but that will also not buy into male-talk like, "I don't do that touchy feely stuff," or "I don't like to talk about my feelings," or "what good will it do?"

It is so paradoxical. Men want to be in rewarding, loving and fulfilling relationships, that is, intimate relationships; yet we do the very things that will insure we won't get there. Because the way to get there is to let go of the resistance to allowing your partner into your heart. And this is exactly what a relationship offers ... the opportunity to let go of fear-based resistance and in the process gain true emotional security and growth.

HOWEVER ... and here is a caveat, and it is a big one. There is a risk. If the relationship is not one that is safe, if it is based on old notions of right/wrong, or tit-for-tat, then going for intimacy is not likely to be a rewarding experience. In fact, your fears will most likely be realized. Make sure your partner is one who wants intimacy and desires the kind of interpersonal connection that it brings. Make sure they want a relationship spelled out in the definition above. Me? I want what *intimacy* provides. It is an apple squarely in the middle of my bowl.

🍎 **Passionate (emotion, feeling); passions (plural):** *the emotions as distinguished from reason; intense emotion; a state of or capacity for emotional excitement; ardent affection; a strong liking for or devotion to some activity, object, or concept; an object of desire or interest: something that commands one's love or devotion; synonyms: Fervor, Ardor, Enthusiasm, Zeal.*

As the third leg of the *Loving* triumvirate (the other two being *Commitment* and *Intimacy)*, this one makes a valuable contribution to my notion of the relationship I want to be in. It is the fuel; the thing that produces the charge ... it is where the fire resides. It is usually the quickest to develop and serves for many as the magnet that pulls them into the more complex relationships. It is also the component that is most at risk of dwindling to an irrelevant status over time. In fact, this is so common that our cultural expectation is that it is a given, it is automatic, that it **will** happen.

We described at the outset of this book how our friends and family, seeing how happy and in love we were, warned that we should enjoy it while we could because it would not last. I am here to tell you that love and passion need not die out. Its dwindling is not a given in my book and I have no expectation that it will be. Quite the opposite.

I like being passionate, and I like being in a passionate relationship. I like the "state of or capacity for emotional excitement." I enjoy the "ardent affection" I have for Bobbie, and she for me. She clearly "commands my love *and* my devotion." And I want to keep it that way. I am *committed* to it. (By now you should be getting a sense of the interplay, the synergy between the apples.)

The positive and powerful emotion that I feel when I am with or think about Bobbie, the excitement, the sense of devotion and desire, are what knocked me off my stool when we first bumped into each other. There are all kinds of theories about where that first rush, the attraction, the desire, the draw comes from.

Maggie Scarff in her book *Intimate Partners* says that it happens when we have awakened within us feelings that take us back to our earliest experience of a time when we felt safe, secure, nurtured, loved ... when all was right with the world. When this happens, we resonate at a very deep level with the person who has stimulated that unconscious recollection.

Scientists have been studying these phenomena in earnest for years. Recently they have posited that our feelings of desire and passion are caused by the complex activity of hormones, neurotransmitters and other substances, such as dopamine, serotonin, and oxytocin.

The earlier musings of Maggie Scarf are in no way inconsistent with the emerging biological model of love and romance. They are actually complimentary, with the scientists giving us a good explanation of what that phenomenon is that the good Dr. Scarff refers to as "resonating."

And that is really good news because it truly casts doubt on the old cultural wisdom referred to earlier that says you cannot keep the romantic, passionate feelings going in perpetuity. The fact is, you can maintain those feelings if that is the kind of relationship you want to be in and your behaviors are consistent with that desire. Because what the scientists tell us is that such behaviors are what create and re-create those feelings, that passion.

Passion is a hallmark of the feelings that were running rampant early in my relationship with Bobbie. I did not have to consciously *do* anything to have the relationship *be* one with a healthy modicum of passion ... and I loved it. And I want it to continue ... so you bet, it is an apple of prominent importance.

◑ **Connected:** *to join, fasten, or link together usually by means of something intervening.*

It might seem a bit redundant to single out *connected* as a specific element of my ideal relationship, given all of the apples that I have included. You might think that the end result of all those apples would be a relationship that *is* connected, one in which the partners are *joined.* My experience is that you can never be too specific and by doing so I am going to give *being connected* high priority. I want to be joined, linked to Bobbie, emotionally and spiritually not just when I am in her presence, but at all times. It is the *connectedness* in the relationship that gives it the substance, that tensile strength, the mass to hold the other apples.

I don't see how a great relationship is possible in the absence of connectedness. How can it be intimate, loving and truly seamless without being connected? It can't. It can be a lot of things, but not these.

It is really fascinating to me to observe those who verbalize a strong desire for *connection* with and to their partner and yet do the most remarkable things that insure the fracturing of any existing connectedness. Having been a great disconnecter in past relationships, I know of what I speak.

The *sticks* conversation in Chapter 3 is all about disconnecting. You want to disconnect from your partner? Pull out the sticks. You want to be in a *connected* relationship? Make sure you get rid of those sticks. Because each time they come into play they weaken the binding we call connectedness until it begins to fray. Ultimately, if the sticks are left untended, the connection will tear irreparably and be permanently lost. At this point, the partners have sunk into the lump-along category and may well be on their way to being an ooots.

I have no idea why anyone would want to be in an unconnected relationship, unless they are consciously putting on the brakes to limit the possibilities. Now, I know that I keep asking this question ... and I am going to do it again. Why would anybody put on the brakes? Why would anybody want to limit the possibilities? Why would anybody want a lump-along relationship at best, and at the worst, induction into the legion of the ooots?

Simply put, do you want to be in a great relationship? Then commit to being connected to your partner and do what it takes to make that happen. The *doing* part of the equation will be dealt with in more detail in Chapter 7.

● **Inclusive: (*enclosing, encompassing*);** *broad in orientation or scope; covering or intended to cover all.*

If I want to be in a relationship with unlimited possibilities, it must of necessity be *inclusive*. This means I must be open to new ideas, new ways of thinking and being. If I am not, but instead hold to a picture of how the relationship should be based on the limits of my personal, narrow view of what works in interpersonal relationships, then I am headed for the ooots camp.

By the way, everybody's personal view is limited and narrow. That's what makes it personal. It comes from the limits of our experience, which is precisely what makes it limiting and narrow.

Relationship is a team sport; it requires the full participation of both parties to achieve its potential and possibilities. I want to include Bobbie in everything I can ... I want her company because I love and enjoy her, but I also want her input, her thinking—her addition, if you will, as well. She is the person I have chosen to spend my life with, and she has chosen me. Why would I want to exclude her and the possibility of growth that she brings to the relationship and thus to me?

Without consciously articulating the desire to have my relationship be inclusive, I run the risk of trivializing and excluding my partner. I have done it in the past and have no desire to do so with Bobbie.

Bobbie and I have worked with a number of couples where one or, at times, both partners feel excluded from the life of the other. And it is usually because they are. You have seen these relationships. Perhaps you are in one. They are easy to identify. They are the ones that are self-described as having "just grown apart," or ones in which "we lead separate lives."

Why would anyone settle for anything less than inclusiveness? Whose idea of a good relationship is that? Not mine. I neither want to just grow apart nor lead separate lives. So, I vote for *inclusiveness*.

● *Expansive (expand): to spread out, open wide; to increase the extent, size, number, volume, or scope of; to express fully, develop in detail; to become larger; may indicate any enlarging by opening out, spreading, unfolding, extending, or increasing.*

For a host of reasons I was not much of a student in high school. I packed the gear to be able to do well, I just didn't. My parents, somewhat baffled, sent me off to a small boarding school in California. Very smart move. It saved my academic life.

There I encountered a wonderful chemistry teacher I remember fondly for two unrelated utterances. Mr. Schuyler told me that he would recommend me to any college in the country, as long as I promised him I would never take chemistry once I got there. The second, and far more to the point of this apple, is a statement he was fond of trotting out whenever he felt the time was appropriate: "Things either expand or contract. If they are doing neither, they are dead." This came to be known as *Schuyler's Rule.*

He was a very wise man. If I remembered nothing else from my encounter with the mysteries of chemistry, I remembered those two things. The former undoubtedly saved me from hours of academic misery, while the second is making a valuable contribution to the success of my marriage and partnership with Bobbie.

Relationships will either expand or contract. When they do neither, they are either dead or dying. One does not need to be a brilliant academic to see this. It makes intuitive sense. A relationship that is contracting is closing in on itself, decreasing the extent, size, number, volume or scope of itself. In essence it is offing itself, committing suicide.

This process is clearly at odds with the notion of an unlimited relationship, and for me it conjures up pictures of silence, withdrawal, strangers passing in the night with less and less expressed between them. When there is conversation, it is couched in feelings of apathy and hopelessness.

At this point the life has most likely gone from the relationship, and it is time for a post mortem. If they are still a couple, they are easy to spot. Kate Winslet in the movie *The Eternal Sunshine of the Spotless Mind* labeled these relationships the "dining dead." They are the ones who will sit through a meal saying nothing and failing to acknowledge the presence of one another.

Committing to being in an expanding, inclusive relationship means you are calling for a vital, active and dynamic one that is constantly a work in progress. Understanding that you never arrive at a stopping point in the development of the unlimited relationship, that it is always something to move toward, is what keeps it alive and vital. When you believe that you have finally "arrived" at THE relationship and can now ease back on the throttle, you are calling for the relationship to contract, which will in turn lead to its demise. An expanding relationship is one that is continually revitalized by new input, new stimuli, thoughts and ideas. And this is necessary if the relationship is to grow and remain relevant.

This concept was made clear to me toward the end of my graduate program. Well along in my career in advertising, I left a very secure job (as secure as you can be in the advertising business) as senior vice president of Hawaii's largest advertising agency and headed out to the University of Texas at Austin to get my doctorate. A fabulous experience.

I loved the program and the city of Austin ... so much so that I entertained thoughts of not returning to Hawaii. I had visions of joining the faculty at Austin and setting up a small private clinical practice. When I shared this with my mentor she said that would never happen. It wasn't that I wouldn't be qualified. In fact, the University would never even consider my qualifications because they had a policy of not bringing someone into the faculty who had been trained at the University. They wanted the benefit of recruiting folks who were trained elsewhere and who would bring different perspectives to the faculty. Bringing someone on board who was trained in their system was not consistent with an expanding, vital and relevant training program. It was more consistent with the development of an "old-boy" networking system, one that is a closed loop, receiving only internal feedback and missing the benefit of outside stimuli and points of view.

I am thankful for their policy. The training I received as a student reflected the vitality of the program, and I certainly benefited from the outside input provided by the heterogeneous faculty. It insured that my training would be relevant, with exposure to a wide and varied body of knowledge.

And being in an expanding relationship serves the same purpose. It provides the context for inter- and intrapersonal growth. It is the training ground that can prepare us to be relevant, vital and contributing world citizens. In contrast, a contracting relationship that slowly unplugs from external stimuli and shuts in on itself serves to maintain singular points of view, rigid ways of being, and inattention to the needs of others in the service of insuring that our own needs are met.

It is really important to understand the difference and distinction between the relationship and those that are in the relationship. I can personally present myself in the world as an open, inclusive and expanding individual while not being that way in my relationship. If I say I want be in an expanding relationship, then my behavior needs to be consistent with my stated desires. That is, I need to be inclusive, supportive and expanding with my partner if I want the relationship to remain alive and vital. Likewise, committing to and supporting an expanding relationship can transform my personal life. And here's the kicker:

By supporting and committing to an expanding relationship *I* continue to expand and grow; by contrast, supporting and remaining in a contracting relationship insures that *I* will contract, shut down on myself, and manifest all those characteristics consistent with contracting, until the relationship can no longer contract.

At this point, Schuyler's Rule rules: Things either expand or contract. Those that do neither are dead or dying.

Merrill's corollary to this is: If I am in an expanding relationship, I will expand. If I am in a contracting relationship I will contract. If I am in a relationship that is dead or dying, I am dead or dying.

So it seems to me that I really have only two choices: Either commit to being in an expanding relationship or do not be in a relationship. Any other choice commits me to an entropic existence. Not a difficult choice. I want what most people want. For certain, I want an expanding relationship.

The question has been asked many ways in many different studies and surveys, and what most people identify as the thing they want most when all the trappings are stripped away is a meaningful, nurturing and close relationship with a significant other.

Me too. And I do not want to be in the dead or dying category. So for certain, I want it to be one that is expanding.

● **Seamless Communication: Seamless:** *having no seam: Synonyms: generous, beneficent.* **Communication:** *ready to give information freely; free, unguarded, and open in conversation.*

Bobbie and I are fortunate. We like each other. And we like to talk to each other. I don't think we are a particularly unique couple ... or at least, we shouldn't be. You would think that most people who say they love their partner would like them and want to talk with them. Wouldn't you? But that doesn't seem to be the case. In fact, it seems to be the exception rather than the rule. Granted, the people that we see in relationship counseling are usually dealing with a deteriorating partnership and want to know what to *do*. This is the time when we will hear the we've-just-grown-apart or we-don't-communicate explanations for the problems. So, they want the cure ... how to grow back in love or how to better communicate.

There is an entire industry built on the notion that we can teach you what to *do* to improve your ability to talk to each other. Active listening, exercises to show your partner you heard what they said, learning to take turns and share the air space, etc., are all derivatives of this industry. And while they might make you feel heard, they do not necessarily have anything to

do with communicating at the level needed to transform relationships, and they certainly do not get to the core of *seamless
communication.*

When I say "talk with" my partner I don't mean idle chatter ... time filler ... surface conversation. I mean communication with my partner for the purpose of making my
relationship as good as I possibly can. Most people do not
have difficulty remaining on the surface in their communication ... we have all sorts of devices to keep us afloat and for
avoiding any deep plunges. There are not many skill-building
exercises that will take you to the depths found in seamless
communication. Because, again, the exercises do not have
anything to do with *being* a communicator, they are all about
doing communication.

As the definition connotes, *seamless communication* requires
a transparency and willingness to remove the self-serving limits that have become a part of our everyday interpersonal interactions. By operating from a definition that calls for freedom,
unguardedness and openness I am signing up for a relationship
in which I neither withhold nor wait to be asked for information, and I am truthful and generous with my communication.
It means I am proactive, positive, and gentle. I am also responsible for making certain the communication is generous, kind
and beneficent ... and I am responsible for the consequences of
what I say.

This is a tall order in a culture that rewards the politic.
Untruths, half-truths, white lies, and denials are all important
in the art of being right and looking good. But they have not
served me well, and I have learned that they have absolutely no
place in relationships ... any relationships. Coming at it from
another angle, why would I want to be anything but seamless
in my communication with my partner? The answer is not that
we don't want to communicate seamlessly, but that it is difficult to *do.* If however, I really adopt this notion of the apples

and am committed to the kind of relationship I want, then the behaviors will follow.

I think it worth repeating again that we are not saying there is nothing to *do*. There is. But it has to be prefaced by clearly articulating, understanding and being firmly committed to the kind of relationship in which I wish to *be*.

⬤ **Safe:** *freed from harm, injury, or risk; no longer threatened by danger or injury*

While physical safety is certainly a part of this apple, it is not what I am referring to here. For me to even begin thinking about being in a relationship with seamless communication, honor, honesty, and passion, it has to be an emotionally and intellectually safe relationship; safe for me and safe for Bobbie. Because if it is not, if it is not free from harm, injury or risk, if it is threatened by danger or injury, true intimacy cannot develop.

Revisit the definition of intimacy. It calls for the revealing of the innermost character, the genuine core, "a warmly personal attitude" that is developed through long or close association by friendliness, unreserved communication (read *seamless),* mutual appreciation and interest. A safe relationship provides the space for this to occur. In essence, being in a relationship that is *safe* allows us to be vulnerable; it allows me to expose my fragility and vulnerability in ways that are impossible in the absence of safety.

Underneath or behind our presentation—the person we want others to see and like—we are *all* fragile and vulnerable. And we perform a variety of psychological sleights of hand to keep it a secret. But in so doing, we miss out on one of the most powerful, rewarding and satisfying aspects of Relationship. We miss the experience of someone really knowing and getting who we are and loving that person in entirety. In a relationship absent safety, our partner will only be getting a partial picture of who we are.

While it may please them—and in fact they may be attracted to and love that partial presentation of our selves—it really *isn't* who we are. *So, if our partner is only experiencing a part of us and that is who they love, we can never experience being fully loved.*

A truly safe relationship allows the intimacy that is necessary for me to be able to present my whole self, warts and all, and in so doing experience being fully loved. If I am in a safe, intimate relationship it also allows me to risk it all and experience loving my partner fully. And that is the essence of the relationship described by Goethe in the *Commitment* conversation above. It is the brass ring we grab on the relationship merry-go-round, the grand prize. And there is no second prize. You either get it all or you run the risk of heading to the ooots camp. Me, I want it all.

◓ *Sexual: of, relating to, or associated with sex as a characteristic of an organic being; involving sex; of or relating to the sphere of behavior associated with libidinal gratification.*

A very important apple for me and one that, while it does not need a whole lot of explanation, should be clearly articulated here, just as it should be in your relationship. I am going to address this from my point of view, so I will be talking primarily to the men who are reading this section.

Now, this might be old hat to some of you. But some do find it to be an area that is difficult to grasp. I can understand that, in that it took me a while to figure it out. Understand that *sexual* is not to be confused with *sex*. While there is certainly an overlap, *sex* is something you *do* or *have* while *sexual* is something you are … or are not … it is the being part of the equation. Webster gets close to it saying that is "related to," but does not say how.

A sexual relationship affords the opportunity for connectedness, a sharing of oneself, being with another in a very unique and intimate way, a way with demonstrable health and psychological benefits. It can be like money in the bank when experienced as warm and bonding, and can carry you and the relationship over the speed bumps that otherwise might derail you. Be clear that sex is not intimacy. It can be intimate, but it is by no means automatic. Just because we know what to do with our anatomy does not mean we know how to be sexual.

We have the cognitive and emotional capacity to be intimate, whereas lower ordered animals do not. It is another one of the things that distinguishes and differentiates us. While many prefer to simply have sex with their partner, I submit they are missing an opportunity to experience themselves, their partner and their relationship in a far more connected way than those further down on the food chain.

For those of you who are holding out for simply being stimulus-response machines and wonder "why should I want to do anything different?" the response is, first, it is not a matter of *doing* anything. It is a matter being ... being intimate, being tender, being caring, being responsive, being loving, being connected, honest, communicative, and so forth. In other words, it is a matter of connecting with your partner with *ALL* of your apples right there with you, holding nothing back.

Interestingly, how we are in our relationship is often reflected in our sexual relationship and vice versa. A successful sexual relationship is not simply a matter of showing up, any more than a successful overall relationship is simply a matter of showing up.

If you are one of those who think that it is, ask your partner if they are satisfied with this aspect of your relationship. My hunch is that their response will tell you why you should want to be *sexual*. It also might give you some idea why you might be experiencing some difficulty in other aspects of your partnership.

🍎 ***Humor:*** *the faculty of perceiving and appreciating the humorous;*

Not much to say here about humor. I start with a real bias. Can't imagine being in a humorless relationship. It would be deadly. So, I want to just give you some random thoughts and observations that I came up with when I was thinking of making this one of my relationship apples.

Some of my fondest highlights (we will talk about highlights in detail in chapter 7) are of Bobbie's smile breaking into a wide grin with the sound of uncontrollable laughter ringing in my ears. We have shared some hilarious moments together, and certainly our similar senses of humor, sometimes perverse, have carried us through some difficult moments.

There is something about humor and the ability to see the nuances of the absurd in everyday events that keeps things in perspective ... and that is something that is sorely needed in our world today. Humor and laughter have been demonstrated to be palliative ... it is good for you and those around you. It is humor that brings the spontaneity and aliveness to the relationship. It contributes to the patina, the texture and robustness and allows us to truly enjoy the fullness and richness of our relationship and our lives. Having and being with someone who has a sense of humor also allows us to truly appreciate the tragedies that we are bound to encounter.

The degree to which you can see and appreciate the humor in situations is the degree to which you can truly connect with and appreciate others. You don't have to be a stand up comic to have *humor* as an integral part of your relationship. All you have to do is be willing to let go of the idea that everything is so significant. That doesn't mean that you and your life aren't significant. It is just that it doesn't have to be that way all of the time. So, lighten up and bring some humor into your life, the life of your significant other, and your relationship. You AND your relationship will live longer.

⬤ *Integrity: an unimpaired or unmarred condition; an uncompromising adherence to a code of moral, artistic, or other values; utter sincerity, honesty, and candor; avoidance of deception, expediency, artificiality, or shallowness of any kind; the quality or state of being complete or undivided: material, spiritual, or aesthetic wholeness.*

I think very few would argue that a relationship should not be one of integrity. And most would argue that they see themselves as individuals of high integrity. I know that I do. I hold my integrity as something that is just not negotiable ... and in scrutinizing the definition, I am aware that I do not always remain in integrity.

And this is an important point for folks to keep in mind in working with the apples: as we have said before, they are aspirational *and* we are human. We will miss the mark from time to time. That is not an excuse for relationship-destructive behaviors. We don't get to say "I can't help it," or "I didn't know." Because we can always help it and now that you have read this far in the book you do know. All we can do is stay conscious of and committed to the apples, fully acknowledging in the moment when what we do is not consistent with what we have committed to ... each and every time we do it.

So, what does it mean to be in a relationship built on integrity? If it is something that you are openly committing to, it means that as a person you are going to show up for your relationships with your best game, your best self. Always.

It means that you are committing to interaction in the relationship at a very high level. It means that no matter what, you will treat your partner with utter sincerity, honesty and candor. It means that when disagreements occur or when you have been called on your behavior, you will *always* take the high road, avoiding the relationship killers of deception, expediency, artificiality or shallowness. You are committing to be fully engaged with your partner and that he or she will always be able to count on the person you are presenting yourself to be; that your partner knows your values and can absolutely depend on and trust you to reflect those values.

Bobbie's Apples

I was more naïve about what was needed to make a primary partnership work than I had realized. By the age of 60 when Tommy and I reunited, I had sorted out my personality to the point that I was pretty happy with myself. As a result I honestly believed that should I meet a partner who was a comparable match to who I had *become* all I had to do was show up, and we would quite easily live happily-ever-after. I had no idea that the happily-ever-after might be more of a challenge than I was predicting, even to couples who are mature, well matched and deeply in love.

Consequently, my apples grew in new and wonderful ways as a result of our joint effort to learn to live with each other in a manner that matched our highest dreams for ourselves and our lives together. I learned that the key was learning to hold fast to being the person I had become and wanted to continue to be in the midst of our bumping into each other's personalities.

This is the most important challenge each couple will face, so learning to select, develop, own and then steadily *be* your particular apples is critical to the success of this process and your partnership.

Although Tommy has so powerfully shared what his apples mean to him and how he carries each one in his *being* and heart, I will explain how some of my most important apples developed in the midst of the pushes and pulls of an actual primary partnership. I will also show how keeping various apples in place helps to support the stability of the other apples.

My commentary will further demonstrate how our various fears and the ways we defend and protect ourselves can cause us to use unclear strategies for living that don't give us what we want. It will also show how developing apples that serve our higher, clearer selves will offer us better guidelines and results.

⬤ **Commitment** was the first of my apples to be confronted and developed and was surprisingly the hardest one for me to understand and adopt. I had assumed myself to be a committed person, loyal to a long-term marriage, raising children, enjoying long-term friendships, participating on sports teams, and developing a full career including some sizable projects, a position as a newspaper columnist and the author of two books. I was one who stuck-it-out along with the best of them, and I assumed I was good at *commitment.*

Yet, under closer examination, *commitment* was not really a strength of mine but had in fact become a weakness. This happened as a result of my staying longer than I should in past relationships, jobs and friendships, leaving me with some questions about the value of *commitment.* As a result of this pattern of dedication to situations that proved hurtful to myself, I had come to view committing as throwing away the key-to-escape during those times when my friend's or partner's apples had gone missing from our relationship bowl and it was no longer appropriate for me to stay.

But once Tommy and I developed the Model, I was able to better gauge the appropriateness of a situation and assess how I should respond. And by using this new relationship standard for my own behavior I could see that *commitment* to *making a relationship work* is very different than *promising to stay, even when apples are missing from the bowl.* Although I had previously failed to grasp how to deal with missing apples while remaining *committed,* the Model clarified how I could keep an eye on the apples as a way to determine if the *commitment* I had made to a relationship was being honored or if the thing I had *committed* to was no longer there.

Thus although making a full and robust *commitment* is critical to the success of any primary partnership, staying in a relationship persistently lacking its agreed-upon apples is no longer appropriate. Once I understood this, I no longer viewed *commitment* as throwing away the key to my on-going ability to assess and choose. And once I felt free to reconsider if needed, making a *commitment* no longer felt dangerous. In fact with the Model to guide me, it not only felt safe, I could now see how important real commitment is to the success of a partnership, and I became eager to give my unrestrained *commitment* to Tommy and our marriage.

However, before I was able to wholeheartedly do this I had to face another aspect of my personality that I had not noticed until I began to more consciously confront my desire to so fully offer my own *commitment* to someone I loved and the partnership we had formed. This second barrier to full *commitment* was an internal dialogue of non-commitment that I had developed early in life which had handicapped my ability to *be* fully *committed* in any of my relationships.

I was first made aware of this barrier to commitment by the gift of *commitment* Tommy so generously gave to me from the beginning of our relationship. His *commitment* came early and raw without any caveats and was the thing that stole my heart and disabled my ability to use my earlier non-commitment tactics of dimming down my feelings for him or thinking of others as I had previously done anytime I was feeling insecure or in disagreement with those I loved.

This tactic of dimming down my feelings for someone unwilling or unable to act consistently loving toward me, and then finding their quick replacement was first set in motion during my childhood. It developed as a result of living with parents who offered me a wonderful and happy home, while simultaneously overlooking my value in favor of their focus on the greater beauty and gifts of my siblings. This early experience of having my value ignored engendered a deep imprint or congregate within me of feeling overlooked, misunderstood and of less value and importance than others. It was a feeling that was subsequently repeated on various occasions throughout my life as early imprints tend to do. And because of this repeating pattern, I felt a need to find a way to protect myself from its pain.

Ironically, one of these times happened during the period in junior high when boys like Tommy Merrill and others failed to notice me in favor of the more attractive girls. In fact, it was in reaction to these experiences that I developed the protective skill of "not caring" and quickly kicking these people out of my heart in favor of others more attuned to my value. Although this skill was initially used to protect me from the sting of rejection, once braces had corrected my crooked teeth and I no longer needed to fend off the hurt of rebuffs in relationships, the mechanism remained stubbornly in place. As a result, starting with my first high school romances, anytime someone did not please me, even for a moment, I immediately rejected them in my mind, if not openly, and then quickly "got over" it and replaced them. This kept me outside of all my relationships, safe from hurt, but also safe from the joys of deep connection that the gift of *commitment* I was finally able to give to Tommy allowed me to experience.

Once I was able to resolve my fear of basic *commitment,* I realized that the most important way to honor my love for Tommy and his love for me would be to give him this deeper level of my *full commitment,* since being in a primary partnership without wholly promising my heart would be the greatest form of partnership betrayal and dishonoring. Because much of my life had been about protecting myself from the pain of such betrayal and dishonoring, I had a profound understanding of what this gift of commitment truly meant. Consequently I felt duly victorious in my triumph over my fears and freedom to so fully and unequivocally offer this gift to Tommy.

Now that *commitment* is securely in place … it serves as my guide for returning me to our relationship during those times when my insecurities and previous urge to bolt are triggered. And in this returning I now *commit* 2,000 percent of my attention to how *I* can make our relationship the best it can be versus merely staying. Thus, rather than dig deeper trenches, putting Tommy on the defensive and myself on the run as I have done in the past, *being* a deeply *committed* partner guides me to turn and face our relationship as the most important thing in my life … and, rather than waver, to put all that I have into making it the best it can be.

In doing this, I strive to be the first to give everything available within me to our relationship without holding anything back or waiting for Tommy to begin. I not only give as much as I know how, but find the courage to bring forth everything I feel might help to repair any drifting, uneasiness or rifts I sense developing between us. I am wholeheartedly *committed* to being my very best and to both *be* and *do* all I can to make our partnership the best it can possibly be. In short, I am inspired by my own pledge of *commitment* to override my early programming of wanting to protect my heart and defend against hurt. My constant goal is to always remain steady in my gift of full *commitment* to Tommy as a way to honor the depth of my love for him as well as the gift of *commitment* he offered me when we first met and so steadfastly continues to give me.

🍎 The next apple that represents the kind of partner I want to *be* and the kind of relationship I want to be in is **Honoring**. This apple first came to my awareness when Tommy shared his encounter with the doctor who so unabashedly honored his wife, and Tommy committed to doing the same with me. I had already experienced the benefits of his desire to honor me and felt he had actually begun this way of *being* in our relationship long before the doctor helped him to identify it as a conscious goal. When he later placed *honoring* at the core of the Model, I joined him in holding it as the centerpiece of all our interactions with each other.

From this experience I realized that by consciously remembering to hold Tommy daily in my mind and heart with an acute awareness of how much I see the genius of his gifts, cherish his good heart, and am in awe of how deeply he loves life and God and me, I am not only moved to treat him with awe and respect, but my feelings of love for him deepen, rather than dwindle. This is the power of consciously committing to *honoring* our partners.

As a result of this daily, conscious focus, *honoring* Tommy has become such a part of who I am that even brief moments of not focusing on the best of who he is feels jarring and out of alignment. And just as Tommy has placed *honoring* at the core of his Model, *honoring* is at the core of my apple bowl. This means considering his preferences and needs at all times, as well as how my attitudes, thoughts, and decisions will impact him and our partnership. But most of all it includes my willingness to keep all of my apples in the bowl at all times and to never yo-yo any of them out for any reason or under any circumstances. As a result, if one of them wanders out of the bowl, even briefly, I am quickly clanged awake by the disharmony of being out of alignment with who I want to *be* and immediately seek to bring it back. This comes more naturally and easily as a result of my commitment to *honor* Tommy.

⬤ **Including** is a critical apple for me. One of the ways Tommy honors me is by his enthusiastic desire to *include* me in all aspects of his thoughts, his decisions, his activities and his life. Like so many others, the thing I have missed and wanted most in my life has been to be seen and valued enough to be embraced and included in this way. When I didn't get this in my youth, I learned to be the hostess to others and to be the one to *be* the *includer.* My style for doing this developed into one of "hanging out" in a relaxed and easy manner comfortable to myself and seemingly to others, including my children and their friends. It is something Tommy also enjoys doing with me. We bring this combination of ease, humor, naturalness and play to all that we do, whether it is work or play, and it is in this way that Tommy *includes* me and I him.

As a result of our easy enjoyment of each others' company and so generously and abundantly *including* the other in all that we do, we are blessed by the synergy that comes out of this sharing of ourselves. The interactions we have enjoyed together as a result of this *including* have led to many moments of great insight, joy and laughter, and we have developed creative projects and become business partners as a result of it. *Including* can generate powerful experiences of comfort, connection, enjoyment and creativity that cannot be experienced without it. *Including* serves as the glue of a relationship, and I can no longer imagine being in one without it.

❂**Seamless Communication** is a unique apple I discovered during the decade I swam in the wild with dolphins and whales throughout the world. The first time the dolphins swam up to me and peered into my eyes for a prolonged period of locked-on gazing, two portals opened for me. One led to an awareness of what an endlessly seamless container the ocean is, a giant basin without walls or doors filled with billions of gallons of water and gloriously decorated with light and color. The second showed me that the kind and caring dolphins seem to have developed an equally seamless and open culture within the context of their seamless and watery world ... and that it includes an intuitive, telepathic awareness of the feelings and thoughts of each other. Because the dolphins made it clear that they could also understand my thoughts, an observation supported by cetacean research, I was inspired by my awareness of this possibility to practice the idea of living in my own culture as if my fellow humans could understand my thoughts as well.

● This led me to a new level of *honesty* and cleaning up who I am in the privacy of my mind and heart. As a result, *full* **Honesty** at it's highest level became a key apple for me and is one of the ones I hold most dear. In using it, I have learned that I much prefer this way of living to hiding my judgments and then denying and defending these lesser parts of myself whenever others get a glimpse of them. This matches the obvious notion that God's security video is on at all times. And once this occurs to us, the idea holds our feet to the fire of truly *being* who it is we want to *be*. As a result of practicing keeping my private self as clean and clear as I could manage for the decade I spent with the dolphins and whales and my continued practice of this, I have become surprisingly more comfortable with who I *really* am and feel free to expose all parts of myself, even though they are imperfect. As a result, I invited Tommy to see all aspects of me when we were first dating, rather than allow him to see only my public presentation. To my delight, he not only appreciated the opportunity to see the real me as voluntarily revealed from the outset, but embraces the concept of full exposure and openness for himself as well.

● Knowing the *Seamless Communication* and *honesty* apples are in our bowl helps us in our mutual goal to be open and free with who we truly *are,* rather than strive to hide or defend the less developed and imperfect aspects of ourselves. This supports our desire to be **Transparent**, rather than right and thus bypass defended interactions and communications. Instead we strive to be open, exposed and raw and to communicate in Side-By-Side conversations, rather than "Crossfire" debates, in the service of getting to an expanded understanding of each other. Since successful communication (discussed further in Chapter 7) is the thing that will ultimately make or break a relationship, the *seamless communication* and *honesty* apples serve as an important foundation for our success in this arena.

☻ Because the *seamless communication* and *honesty* apples in our bowl also serve as the foundation to **Integrity**, if they are in place so will *integrity* be. It becomes automatic, since any-time our truths are known and can be counted on, our partners are able to trust who is genuinely present in the relationship with them … and from the moment they feel they can trust this, whatever we do and say can be believed. This has impact-ed our relationship at its core and has been both healing and building for both of us.

☻ Our *integrity* apple inspires great feelings of relief and an enormous sense of **Safety** with each other. This kind of safety in our relationship allows both of us to surrender and relax and feel even more *transparent* and open with each other.

☻ If I then use what Tommy exposes to me as an opportunity to further understand and love him, rather than debate, judge, correct or control him, I am in a unique position to offer him the most precious gift of all, the gift of **Understanding.** This includes my willingness and ability to see and value him as he truly is—both the depths of his gifts that others have over-looked as well as a gentle and kind look at his flaws. Since most of us desire this experience of being so fully seen, understood and loved, it serves as a wonderful gift that we give each other and may fulfill one of the primary purposes of our partnership.

☻ From this place of absolute *safety* and feeling both *understood* and *loved,* all barriers to **Connection** and **Intimacy** are removed, and we are able to enjoy even deeper levels of *love.*

☻ We can also see how our collection of apples help us to feel even more open and safe, which in turn activates strong feelings of **Passion** and a desire for a more *intimate* **Sexual** experience.

◕ Three of the most valued apples for both Tommy and myself include the **Spiritual, Humor** and **Expansive** apples, and for me these are linked by the enormity of their importance to our lives.

We first bonded on a note of *humor,* and it was Tommy's ability to put me into uncontrollable laughter on our first date that put him squarely in my heart and linked me to him for the rest of our lives. Although humor is challenging to describe, shared humor is born out of a shared way of viewing things and is consequently very bonding.

It is a similar sense of shared perception and a mutual love for God that bonds us *spiritually* in a correspondingly moving and joyful manner. And it is this shared experience that serves as the driver of all parts of our lives.

◕ Not surprisingly, it is the combination of all these apples, that keep our lives continuously stretching, reaching and *expanding* in ways that fulfill our lives with the synergy of **More**. As a result, we have succeeded in the goal we set when we decided at the beginning of our relationship not to lower the bar on our expectations for love and happiness, but to *Settle for More.*

You can begin to see how our collection of apples has directed us away from the sticks that might have otherwise picked away at the Velcro of our initial bond. And now that they have been clearly selected and articulated, the apples will serve as steady guides for who we want to *be* and the loving partnership we want to *have.*

WE SAY

The Bowl Is Full

So, that's it. Those are the apples, the things we have included in the relationship we have created for ourselves. If you like them, take them. If you have others that you feel more accurately describe the relationship you want, terrific. Use them.

The point is, *you* create the relationship *you* want.

As we said at the outset of this chapter, the chances of you getting what you want are increased significantly if you know and can clearly articulate to yourself and others what that is. To us, this doesn't take much of a sell.

At this point you might be saying, "Look, I really like the ideas you have in your apples, but the chances of me being able to really put them into practice with my partner or those that I have previously been with are not so hot. And it doesn't seem that the chance of it working for those I know is any better. I can think of all kinds of scenarios that would argue against success."

So can we. And we have probably heard and seen all of the situations you can come up with, plus more. And yet we are certain that if this is something you want—if you want to *settle for more*—then it is *doable*. Notice that we are now introducing the notion that there is a *doing* in this model. Chapter 7 will give you some ideas that we have incorporated into the relationship that will address many, if not all, of your concerns. Onward and upward.

"BE the apple." —TOM AND BOBBIE MERRILL

SECTION 3

Down from the Mountain to Harvest the Dream

EIGHT

The *Doings*

"If we don't live our moments the way we want our lives to be, we can't have the lives we want."
—BOBBIE SANDOZ MERRILL

We enjoy and often refer back to the story of the monk who, after years of meditating up on the mountain, gained enlightenment and returned to the town far below. Aglow with his newly gained sense of universal understanding and the ability to be in the moment, he entered the town to find the hustle and bustle of life going on much as it had before he took off for the mountains and years of contemplation. As he walked towards the center of town, the traffic, people and congestion increased to where he was finding it difficult to get about unhindered.

With a knowing eye he observed the apparent indifference and unconsciousness people seemed to show in their interactions with others as they hurriedly shoved and jostled their way to wherever they were going to or coming from. Then standing at a corner waiting for the "walk" signal to flash, he felt pleased with his ability to remain in his state of reverie and silently thanked the universe for the opportunity he had been given to achieve enlightenment.

At that moment a large gentlemen pushed his way to the front of the curb and in his haste stepped on the monk's sandaled foot, mashing his baby toe. Yanked instantly out of his bliss state, the monk lashed out, and bringing a heavyweight caliber left hook out of nowhere, dropped the brute.

Hmmmmm. So, what's the point? Well, there are several. First, for the past few chapters we have been touting the importance of who we are *being* as the best path to *settling for more* and achieving an unlimited relationship. We have repeatedly, and in a variety of ways, pointed out that it is not what you are *doing* but how you are *being* that counts, since *being* is the beginning of the creating cycle. And due to the importance of this, we have emphatically stated that you can't *do* your way to a great relationship but have to start with the *being* end of the *be-do-have* cycle. To start at the other end is to experience the salmonesque quality of swimming up stream.

In addition, we have been saying that if you know what you want and can articulate and visualize it, you will know who you want to *be* and what relationship you want to *be* in. And once you know what these are, you will have a much better chance of getting them, and that this is the beginning of creating the experience of the relationship in which you want to *be*. We have also said the apples are the vehicle to articulating those things you consider the most important and necessary values and ways of *being* that you will hold yourself and your partner to. We further painted a picture that suggests if you are then committed to a relationship based on your apples, you can venture out into the world of interpersonal interactions holding your apple bowl up for all to see and that by holding your own feet to the fire in this way you will guarantee your success.

It won't. You might well end up having an "enlightened-monk" experience, metaphorically round-housing the first person who crosses you, doesn't play fair, tries to win, makes you wrong or resurrects any of the other sticks that got you into battle in your pre-apple, pre-enlightened stage of life.

About now, you might be saying, "Well, that's terrific! So what good is all of this *being* and apple business?" Good question. The point is that while we may have all the information available on how to make things work, our own stuff will still predictably surface and get in the way. We are trained in it. We have had years of practice at it. We see and mimic the behaviors of unsuccessful relationships all around us ... from our parents, teachers, cinema, television ads, situation comedies, weekly prime-time dramas, novels, our friends' relationships, popular music, political leaders, and so on. From our infancy until this moment, we have been bombarded with images of unsuccessful relationships we have grown to accept as the cultural norm. That is what we know and have always done.

Yet this disconnect between who we say we want to be in our most important and cherished primary partnerships and the way we behave in the privacy of our homes creates a serious problem. For it is this very lack of congruency between what we say and what we do that prevents us from having what we claim to most value and want. And rather than figure out how to keep our apples in the bowl and live by the values we have claimed, we put our energy into defending the many exceptions we make to the standards we have set for ourselves.

It is the same gap created by the values espoused in the *thou shalt* culture and the reality of the way we as a larger humanity behave in the world. And again, rather than figure out how to keep our apples or stated values in the bowl, we focus on defending why they are out.

Although we have said this congruence can only be attained not just by verbalizing, but by deeply embodying the values we claim, you must also understand and practice how to do it. And since we have shown you how to embrace and fully *be* what you claim to want, we will now show you how to *do* it. The key is to remember that the gap can only be closed when both are in place. And when they are, you will experience a wonderful congruence between your highest dreams and your best self. Even more important, that best self will also be congruent with who you are in the world, starting with your partner in your own home.

So now that we know what we want and are willing to raise the bar on what we will accept in ourselves and our relationships, we need to *DO* it differently. Yes, we are now pushing the *doing* part of the *be-do-have* cycle.

Look at it this way. Creating the relationship of your dreams, meditating on it, praying for it, writing daily affirmations ... all of that is terrific. But when it shows up, *you* will still have to *do* relationship. And this is where the rub has always been—and where it will continue to be—if you stick with doing it the old-fashioned way. Thus if you—like the monk—reach back in your repertoire bag and pull out the old dance steps and sticks during those times when you are challenged in your relationship dance, you will be back in the place you were trying to leave.

It would be as if you were a carpenter who had been framing houses for twenty years. But then you decide you want to gain the skills necessary to be a finished carpenter doing fine cabinetry work for custom built homes. So you get the training, show up for your first day on the new job and are asked to install some beautiful cabinetry. You carefully position the woodworking masterpiece into the space allotted, but it does not quite fit. You have all of your fine, finished carpentry tools laid out—expensive, dainty little chisels, fine sandpaper, razor sharp planes—alongside your older, heavy-duty framing tools. After several minutes of trying without success to slide the cabinet into its small place, you reach for the trusty old framing sledge hammer and pound the masterpiece a couple of good ones. Our hunch is that the foreman would either fire you or have you back on the framing crew in nothing flat.

One of the things we know is that when placed under stress, people will regress to those behaviors they experienced as being successful in previously similar situations. If being right is important, they will do whatever they feel worked when their goal was to defend themselves and prove their rightness; or if they feel a need to protect themselves from being ignored or disdained, they will use familiar, though outdated tools, such as withdrawing, in order to avoid feeling discounted.

If you use your old way of being and doing, you will end up back in the ooots and toots piles. But if you use the new *doing* tools presented in this chapter while remaining consistent with the *being* apples you have developed, the outcome will be a relationship that is everything you have envisioned, and perhaps more.

Interestingly, the new behaviors reflecting the person you have chosen to *be* are easy to *do,* easier in fact than the old ones. Much easier. But they will also be new, almost foreign to you at first, and thus not yet habitual. As a result, it will take some time to consciously change over to the new way of *being* and *doing.* Consequently, you might be tempted to entertain the illusion that the new is harder, but that is only because it is new and thus still unfamiliar.

But if your intention is clear, the switch can take as little time as a moment ... or as long as a few weeks or months. And then you are there. Once there, you have raised the bar, and *being* and *doing* the old way will no longer seem familiar, but foreign and increasingly uncomfortable ... while the new way becomes the more familiar, natural and easier road to take.

Some may balk at the idea of changing so fast, since we are unaccustomed to actually acting on the good ideas we read and learn about. This is because we are acculturated to *settling for less,* and the concept of *settling for more* and then getting about the business of doing so is new to us. Yet if you truly choose to raise the bar and make this your intention, you can do it, and we have some tips to help.

To begin, we suggest that you carefully read and absorb the new ways of *doing* presented in this chapter, just as you have read and absorbed the new ways of *being* described in earlier sections. Then, take on the mantle of how this looks and feels, allowing those around you to actually see the apples reflected in your behaviors and interactions. Begin to act on the combination and allow it to fully penetrate who you *are* in your heart and how you *do* things in the world. Begin now, not later. You are almost there, safe from the sticks and the "ooots" and "toots" piles. So read on.

Communication Landmines

The most dangerous landmines that can derail relationships lie in the way we communicate or don't communicate with each other and the degree of understanding or non-understanding we take from these communications. Although we might expect to have our most frequent and rewarding communications occur in our most important and intimate relationships, the reverse is often true. In reality the abundance of our communication errors not only reflects the degree to which we have lowered our bars but serves as rich fodder for our growing twig piles.

The point is, we are no longer on dates, holding hands or engaged in lingering eye contact, nor are we giving the other our full honoring and attention. Instead, we are using shortcuts and without even sitting down or looking at each other, we are now trying to sandwich our most important communications of the day into the activities and chores of our busy lives. This approach causes genuine hurt, followed by defensive reactions such as anger or withdrawing.

As a result of our shift to this more sterile, shorthand approach to communication, we now find ourselves no longer hearing everything said or feeling heard. As a result we are quick to misunderstand and feel misunderstood, followed by frequent disagreements and increased disconnection.

We have no cultural standard for communicating effectively and thus no way to come to accord or resolve our problems. As a result, we spend the majority of our time in gridlock where we remain addled with horns locked and no clue what to do. This leads to our sense that conversation has become dangerous, and we increasingly stick to surface topics dealing primarily with facts and an occasional opinion.

Next, opinions begin to also be viewed as risky, and a discussion of feelings and needs is out of the question. At this juncture, we may retreat to non-solutions such as, "I have nothing to add … so you talk while I listen" or the coldly stated "whatever you say" followed by broader bands of silence.

We have failed as a culture to teach the most basic socializing skills either at home or school. And our failure shows up most clearly in our poor approach to relationship communication. Yet without better skills in this important area of human interaction the best we can offer is to continue our fights or surrender to the common therapeutic suggestion of "agreeing to disagree." This is meant to imply that we have uncovered some place of agreement while getting us out of a communication not going well, but it is clearly more disagreeable than agreeable and leaves us at an impasse, with our closeness and connection lying in the balance.

Without a better way to resolve our differences, we have nowhere to go but further down the road of relationship breakdown. At this point, some will seek the company of new friends of the opposite sex who might better hear and understand them, while others more honestly face the depth of their problems and begin to consider divorce.

But before we get to that point, we start to wonder what happened to the days when we viewed things similarly to our partner and rejoiced in our like-mindedness. How did our most intimate friend become our most zealous sparring partner, now stimulating within both of us an urge to win, rather than relate? And how do we now shift these disconnecting interactions back to effective ways to relate and re-bond?

It seems most relationship breakdowns are seen in our failure to communicate effectively. Yet no matter what the source of the difficulty, good communication offers us our only chance to fix it. We already know this, but we still don't know how.

Others before us have designed an array of methods and tools to fix this most persistent arena of failed human interactions. But so far, nothing has really worked. So the question is, will our approach be the one that can break through and truly help people continue to communicate in the kind, attentive and understanding ways they offered each other during courtship? We believe it will. In fact we believe we have uncovered the first program that can break through this most dangerous threat to continued partnership connection.

A Quick Course in Successful Communication

And so this is where we want to jump in and offer a completely new road with real solutions. We want to wake you up at this point to let you know that you and your partner *can* resolve this.

We also want you to know that if you will study and use the communication style we suggest in the next twenty pages, the change you make will have an enormous impact on your relationship, your family and even the world. We are not exaggerating. We truly believe it.

If each of us can consistently keep our *Communication* and other apples in our bowls while conducting our primary partnerships, then we can do it with our children, our friends, our colleagues and beyond. In truth we are all just a few apples away from having the relationships and lives of our dreams, but we must first learn to use our apples in the midst of being buffeted by the world. In fact, if the monk from the mountain had been carrying his apples and knew how to use them, his reaction to the jostling of the people around him and the toe masher would have been consistent with the person he wanted to *be*.

The first level of this buffeting starts the moment we cross the threshold to be in our own homes with our partners, so this is where we must begin practicing the behaviors that best reflect who it is we want to *be*. If we succeed there, *doing* it in the world will be easy.

This is because by practicing our best behaviors at home, over time they will become a part of us and penetrate who we truly are at our core. Until now most of us have had this backwards and have been practicing our best manners while out in the world and then letting down to our worst selves at home.

And so we will now show you how to convert the *being* you desire into your *doing* in the world. We will begin by showing you how to do your best in your own homes and personal relationships, starting with your partner. And we will start with communication, since it is the primary way we engage and interact with each other. As such, it is the thing that can bond or distance us. And it is the thing we must get right if we want our relationships and world to work.

The Monk's Challenge

Your first challenge—like the challenge of the monk—is to find a way not to react emotionally to something your partner does or says which has the potential to lure you into a polarized position of "me against you." Because of the importance of resisting this temptation, all of our *doing* steps are designed to keep you out of this ready-to-fight frame of mind and point you toward a more rewarding *Side-By-Side* style of communication.

Stay with us on this, for if you understand and use these steps, you can do it. You can blend your *being* with your *doing* and bring your most lofty dreams into the reality of your daily lives, starting in your own homes with your most challenging, yet potentially most rewarding relationships. Interestingly, as unattainable as this seems, it is easier than it sounds and far easier than not doing it. The only reason it seems beyond our reach is because we have never been taught the simple steps that will take us there. So here they are.

BOBBIE SAYS

The Intention to Understand

The best way to keep from being buffeted by the tides of partnership communication is to hold the strong intention of understanding our partners at all times, not just when they are upset with us and we feel a need to more closely attend, but all the time. For if we are clear that our only goal in communication is to steadily understand, all else will fall quite easily—and wonderfully—into place.

So rather than allow this critical aspect of communication to fade from your partnership life, we suggest you reinstate—or activate—your skills as an *understander* and be willing to stick with offering this gift, even if your partner has stopped.

Attending

In order to succeed in the goal of continued understanding, we must remember to carefully attend as we did during courtship, rather than shift to the more careless, non-attentive and interruptive communication style so often used following courtship. So what is the difference?

The thing that most hurts our post courtship communication—and our partner—is an apparent decline in the level of our interest in communicating with them, which is reflected in the very different way we attend. For example, rather than sit down to converse in depth as we used to, often while looking into each other's faces and eyes, we are more likely to do it in shorthand on the run, sometimes with our backs to each other or perhaps even from another room. As a result, rather than create an atmosphere that promotes the same close listening we used to enjoy, we no longer look at our partner, show that we truly care about what is in their heart, and often listen with half an obliged and impatient ear—or even overt interruptions—to their scrambled attempts to share themselves with us.

Moreover, rather than respond with our most considered response, we minimize our contribution to the conversation with abbreviated comments, disagreement with the snippets we have heard or by trivializing what they have shared by offering quick judgments, often expressed by our growing indifference or complete silence.

Our partner is not only humiliated and hurt by this shift, which creates a nick in their heart each time it happens, they are no longer able to impress us with their brightness, wit or charm. And this is because we have withdrawn our intention to keep caring enough about who they are and what is within them to keep attending to them or listening to their thoughts and feelings with the goal of understanding them. In short they have no way to continue to enchant and attract us or be understood by us on an ongoing basis, for we are no longer there with them.

Before long they begin to realize their communications have no opportunity for even minimal success with us, and they too begin to drop out. In time, both partners experience a growing loss of interest in each other which results in even more inattention, misunderstandings and hurt as well as a widening of the gap between them. In some cases, one or both may strive to get the lost attention from others, which makes matters worse.

So what could change this destructive pattern? It's so simple, but rarely done. If post courtship partners would do three things, they could continue to have outstanding communication and a deepening bond between them.

To begin, it's important to make sure all of the apples selected for the partnership are in the bowl at all times—not most of the time, but all of the time. This is because if such things as *Honoring, Kindness, Loving* and *Caring* are included, it would be impossible not to attend, since any one of these apples is incompatible with inattention.

With apples in place, the first step is to discern between those times when we are chatting lightly in the course of living together from those times when we want the *full* attention and attending of our partner. Thus although considerate listening and responding are always important, there are times when we require more careful attending than we do on those occasions when we are chatting and passing in the hall as we dress for the day.

However, what seems to go wrong for couples is that the passing-in-the-hall style of attending increasingly replaces the times that require our full attention. And then at some point it seems the chatting in the hall is all that is left. As a result, it is our conscious return to more careful attending on a daily basis that is needed if we are going to experience a full and robust partnership tooled to expand to it's unlimited potential. In short if we truly want to *settle for more,* we must continue to offer the gift of attending and understanding.

The Second Step is designed to help us accomplish the First Step. The key is to find a way to "hang out" together at least once a day for a relaxed segment of time that is long enough to allow a connection to happen. This is best done by fully surrendering to sitting—or reclining—together somewhere enjoyable to both partners and a feeling of time restraints. It's important that conversation allows each partner an opportunity to openly and completely share thoughts and feelings ... and to offer each other the gift of hearing and "getting" who the other is as they did during courtship. Once a connection is made, both will feel ready to move on to other parts of their day or evening, and doing this paradoxically takes less time than repairing the problems that arise when we don't do it. And so by returning some form of hang out time, not on special occasions or even weekly, but daily, offers couples a chance to remain truly close and in love.

I have taught this same technique to parents to use in their interactions with their children, especially upon their returning home from school. Reports reveal this has produced phenomenal results by assuring children during this bonding time that they are loved, and it works equally well in all relationships in which true bonds and expanded connection are desired. But the key is that hang out time includes *being* and *attending* with the goal of hearing and understanding, rather than the busyness of activities that can actually interfere with attending to the person.

The Third way to protect outstanding communication following courtship is to use the 3-part skill set explained in more detail below of communicating in a *Side-By-Side* manner, with the goal of *Being the Understander* and finding a way, when needed, to get to *The Third Story.*

Side-By-Side Communications

To accomplish *Side-By-Side* communication we must first find a way to by-pass getting emotionally flooded and then becoming defensive or adversarial on those occasions when we feel misunderstood and hurt or confronted, and the desire to defend or flee comes over us. For anytime we feel vulnerable or under siege, most of us get single-minded about finding a way to protect ourselves from our perceived attacker or beating them at their own game. And like the monk, even though we want to remember our apples, we feel most challenged to do so whenever our circumstances feel emotionally chaotic and out of our control.

This is because whether we choose to fight or flee in response to these conditions, our choice comes out of our fear that we will not be understood or respected and that love will be temporarily withdrawn or permanently taken away from us. As a result, our initial desire to listen and communicate now shifts to an interest in not losing. At this point we feel flooded by our emotions, and all we can attend to is our need *not to lose the battle.* In this shift, some of us are blinded by anger and want to strike out while others are frozen in fear and want desperately to escape. Whichever the path our emotions take us, our communication skills are deeply affected and we invariably become paralyzed, clouded and defensive. We also feel a rapid loss of closeness to our partner during these periods, and though we like to assume this loosening of our bonds will tighten again when we make up, in truth these ruptures do not always fully heal unless we take the time to carefully mend them with in-depth conversations or full *Clearing* as explained later.

So if in the middle of feeling so unraveled by our emotions we are able to hold to the goal of getting literally and metaphorically *Side-By-Side,* it will feel to both of us as though we are on the same team, supporting the partnership, rather than on opposite sides, supporting only ourselves. And from this very different and friendly place we will be able to engage in truly effective communications.

If we can also stay with our desire to use the communication to connect, rather than win, we will be more steadfast in our goal of switching from the battlefield where there will be no winners to a *Side-By-Side* interaction. From this safe and friendly position, sitting literally next to our partner, holding his or her hand, we are reminded that we love each other and that our *only* goal is to deeply *hear* and *learn* from the perceptions and information our partner would like to share with us.

Of course it helps if our partner's goal is to also do this from an equally gentle place in their hearts. But it's important that this not be a prerequisite or something we do *only* if our partner has also agreed—and remembered—to do it. This is no time to succumb to the seductive urge for a tit-for-tat exchange. If we have kept *all* our apples in our bowl, we will be sincerely happy to be the first to get Side-By-Side, even if our partner has not yet begun. This willingness comes out of our having already claimed wanting to *be* in a Side-By-Side relationship and *being* a Side-By-Side person, independent of the behaviors of our partner. And by holding to our apples and successfully getting Side-by-Side, even under these more challenging conditions, we stay in charge of who we want to *be* and no longer allow others to choose for us, just because they have chosen differently for themselves.

By taking our own "stuff" off the table, including such things as our personal reaction to being hurt or challenged, we are better able to be who it is we truly want to be as well as more clearly view who it is our partner is. And whether or not we continue in partnership with this particular partner, we have been the first to leave the starter's gate to begin the process of being our best and are thus on our way to both *being* in the relationship we say we want and *doing* what it takes to make this happen. For whatever happens from here, it is ourselves we take with us wherever we go, and it is ourselves who define the kind of relationship we are in. This is your key to happiness, so take a moment to think about it.

Being the *Understander*

I first uncovered the concepts of *Side-By-Side* communication and being the *Understander* in my work with children, which is described in my book on parenting. I rediscovered these as they relate to primary partnerships in a completely new and wonderful way soon after Tommy and I were married. The following example explaining the moment I made this discovery highlights *all* the components needed for a uniquely effective communication between partners actively engaged in the midst of a struggle. Read it carefully, for if you understand the power of how this works, you too will be tooled for effective communication, while keeping your apples in your bowl.

Tommy and I were suddenly in the midst of a "hoo-hoo," and I was dismayed. I had not seen it coming, but something I said upset him, and before I even realized there was a problem, Tommy was speaking to me in tense and frustrated tones. At first I wanted to run from the communication, since I had no idea what had made him feel so upset with me, and like him, I felt quickly discouraged by the process as my emotions became unraveled. But rather than act on my standard urge to escape under such circumstances, I looked at Tommy and watched his face for a while. Because he was angry, he wasn't as clear or bright as he usually is, and when I then challenged what he was saying, it seemed to me he had become even less clear as he got angrier.

I didn't like what was happening to him or to me. And I was concerned that after so many hours of wonderful conversations we had wandered into this land mine. And so I made a deliberate choice to calm down and take my part of this conflict off the table in an effort to more clearly see what remained of this problem and better understand what was happening.

As I continued to watch his face and listen to him talk, I was reminded that his brightness was one of the primary magnets that had drawn my heart into a relationship with him. I also realized in that moment that someone so bright could not have come to the conclusions he had drawn about me in a vacuum, and so I listened more carefully, as I had during all of our earlier, non-emotionally charged conversations. My goal had shifted from protecting myself or claiming my "rightness" to seeing if I could understand how his perceptions and thinking had brought him to this point. When I didn't understand, I gently asked questions, not in a confrontational, opposing manner as I had at first, but with genuine interest as to how his thinking had taken him down this road.

In this moment, I shifted my goal to become the *understander*, rather than strive to be the one *understood*. In response to this change in my goal, I felt soft and loving in my heart, and from this gentler place remembered how kind and loving he had always been with me. This reminded me that I wanted even more to understand and not discount him or his experience. And so rather than keep only speakers in the room with no listeners to hear them, I shifted my mood to one of valuing and honoring Tommy and became a true listener of his words. I then walked across the room to where he was sitting and calmly sat down beside him. In this further shift to an even gentler place within myself, I had brought my apples back into the room and created a *Side-by-Side* atmosphere.

Then rather than interrupt to correct or disagree with the things I was hearing or debate each of Tommy's points as they surfaced, I allowed him the airspace he needed to more articulately and clearly express the larger point he was striving to develop. I then carefully tugged at the tips of the scarves of information he gave me so that I could pull the rest of what was not yet said out into the open for me to see and understand. My new goal was to see if I could genuinely perceive and understand things the way he was perceiving and understanding them. I had no further need to get mired in the accuracies of who said exactly what and when they were said or to engage in the bickering required to get these details corrected. All I wanted at this juncture was to capture the *essence* of the communication and offer Tommy the gift of understanding his perceptions and the points he was making.

As he talked, I had an amazing insight. What had previously seemed like an absurd and irritating idea now made sense to me, and the more I listened the more I actually agreed with him. As a result of my *Side-by-Side* desire to truly listen and hear what he had to say, he was now able to impart to me that I had been doing something completely outside of my own perceptual field. And because the information was initially new and foreign to what I had previously seen in myself, when he first talked about it, I felt misunderstood and wanted to bat the information away and argue that it wasn't true. But now, from my more *Side-By-Side* position and commitment to calm and careful listening, what he was describing actually rang true and added to my fuller understanding of myself and the way I react under certain conditions. I let Tommy know that I could now perceive what he was perceiving and in fact agreed with all but a few small points.

This was a gift of understanding I had given to so many children—so often unheard or understood by the adults in their world—during my years as a child therapist and school consultant. And it was one I had given to thousands of clients and parenting class participants. But it felt even better when I first learned to give it to my own children and now to Tommy, the person I had chosen to be my life partner. For it is in these most intimate and vulnerable relationships that the gift of understanding is the most challenging to give. Yet succeeding during these times also offers some of life's greatest rewards.

It was a unique experience for Tommy, and he was both moved and grateful to be heard in this respectful manner in the middle of a disagreement. He sincerely appreciated the gift of *understanding* I had just given him and began immediately to return the gift and listen more carefully to my perceptions and view. On that particular occasion, we both came away agreeing

more with him than me, but with one of my points also included as an important piece that Tommy had not previously seen
or understood. Yet the real blessing of the interaction was not
only the clarity we were able to achieve, but the gift of *understanding* we had each given to the other, a gift that drew us
remarkably closer.

The *Third* Story

This new way of interacting took us out of a contest to see
which of our opinions was the superior. Instead, we were both
able to perceive more aspects of the picture and gain a broader
understanding of the larger story and each other. Because of
this expanded way of looking at the situation, it became neither his way nor mine, but a *Third Story*, influenced by both
views yet different from both. We liked our *Third Story* and realized it had not come out of one of us winning or the other losing the communication, but represented our dual victory in
acting as *understanders*.

Whenever we use this approach, all feelings of disagreement
between us dissolve, since we are able to see and understand
the other's point of view and how they got to the opinion they
are holding. And once we allow ourselves to see all of the sides
to all of the puzzle pieces that make up a conversation, the
things that previously didn't make sense can now be seen and
understood in the context of the whole.

Yet to get to this point we need to literally sit *Side-by-Side*,
keep the emotion out of the equation, assume the role of
Understander, keep *all* of our apples in the bowl, and take care
not to become polarized or fight to win, but look instead for
The Third Story. With this atmosphere in place, the only
remaining component needed to accomplish a successful communication is an unequivocal commitment to the *Honesty*
apple. For it is during times of challenging communication

when our need to expose even the most subtle nuances of all of our *truths* puts this particular apple to its greatest test.

The following pages will offer you more information on what we did to accomplish this successful communication and how you, too, can do it. Once you grasp the meaning of the next dozen pages and are willing to use it, you will dramatically change all of your interactions with others, starting with your primary partner.

A CLOSER LOOK AT HOW TO DO IT

Because Tommy and I are both therapists with years of practice in listening to clients, we were able to bring strong listening skills to our relationship and were most careful to use them during courtship. As a result of possessing these skills, our only on-going task during times of heated communication has been to keep our *Honesty* and other apples in the bowl while holding our emotions in appropriate check. Whenever we succeed in keeping these components in place, we are equipped with the skills needed to deeply hear and understand each other. And that's what we do. So what are these skills? And can we share them with you? The answer is yes. Can we do it quickly, yet effectively? Yes again. So here they are, the Cliff Notes for highly skilled listening, and the *only* road to true understanding.

Emotion and Communication

Whenever one partner triggers the emotions of the other, some reaction ranging from feeling hurt to getting defensive is set off and the communication is immediately in trouble. Sparks and sticks begin to fly and misunderstandings prevail. If we continue on this road it will clearly lead to problems unless we can interrupt the pattern. So what are some of the things we can do? Starting soft and staying soft will by-pass these problems. Following are some tips for doing this.

A Soft Heart and Gentle Ear

Although your goal will not be to act like a therapist in your primary partnership, it will be to learn to listen like one. This is a skill I teach to families in my parenting classes and explain in my parenting book, and many have reported benefiting from using it. The first step includes learning to listen with a gentle ear from a place of softness in your heart. Although activities such as running, meditation, yoga and prayer help us to find this gentle place within ourselves, they require an investment of time to get there. To counter this delay, I discovered a shortcut to help parents accomplish this more quickly.

To begin, I have parents consider how they would respond in the presence of a frightened bird or lost kitten or puppy. Most can quickly see that their energy would automatically shift to their hearts as they carefully extend their hand in a gesture of making friends and assuring the animal that their hearts and intentions are filled with safety, comfort and kindness.

Presenting this same gentle attitude similarly assures our children—as well as our partners—and anytime we assume this kinder approach with them, they too will feel soft and relaxed in our presence. This inspires them to open their hearts in turn as they feel safe enough to more calmly and articulately express themselves. Although this is simple and solves the problem, most people make it harder than it needs to be. Following are some tips to help you choose this higher road.

Unrung Bells and Pointed Pistols

I was raised in a home filled with many good things and parents who sincerely tried to be their best. Life was unduly rich for a family of such modest means, and I was later fascinated by how my family managed to draw such an abundance of experiences to us.

As was common in those times, I possessed a few well selected and cherished toys, and my favorite of these was a paper doll that I loved to dress in her paper clothes. But one morning, when one of her outfits wouldn't stay fastened no matter what I tried, in a fit of anger I ripped my doll into numerous small pieces. I immediately regretted my deed and began to cry in a way I had never experienced. Yet no matter how much scotch tape I used, I finally had to accept that I couldn't restore her.

And so at the tender age of five, I learned several big lessons. I learned that rage serves absolutely no purpose and that there are bells that can't be unrung no matter how much you regret them. But the best lesson I took from the sting of the first two is that before the doll was destroyed, I had a moment of choice. It's a choice I have since exercised throughout much of my life and a lesson that serves me well when I remember to use it. It's the same choice we make any time we are on the verge of hurting those we love as a result of anger run amuck. And the key to remember is that we always have a choice.

But not everyone shares my paper doll experience or the lessons that went with it, and it seems the majority of couples upset with each other believe that controlling their emotion-driven behavior will be too difficult. In fact most assume it would be impossible. So Tommy asks them what they would do if he was holding a pistol to their heads and would fire it if they exhibited the unwanted behavior? They are always clear that under those conditions, they could do it. So it seems the real problem lies in our failure to really understand the less visible consequences of our partnership behaviors done from an emotionally charged place. Yet if we truly understood the severity of the consequences of the pain we inflict on our loved ones and the impact our angry actions have on their feelings toward us, we would raise the bar on our behaviors and do better. Much better. And we would find it far easier than we think.

But what most of us aren't realizing when we fail to make this effort is that the relationship is permanently altered. We erroneously believe that when the problem du jour has blown over we can pick up where we left off. But this is not true ... especially for women. The battle bells have a way of continuing to ring in their heads and accumulating ... until one day it is over. Men tend not to understand how it gets to the end so quickly for women because men often fail to understand the cumulative effect fighting and anger have on women. It reminds me of my favorite explanation of the course of alcoholism, which will have meaning for anyone who has watched a loved one fall into this abyss. The course goes along for awhile until suddenly one day, the person takes a drink; but the next day the drink takes them. It seems to happen overnight, in the same way the "last straw" and a serious decline in feelings of closeness or even the final dissolution of a person's love for us seems to happen overnight.

Those of you who have been working with your apples will find it easier to select high level choices that reflect the person you truly want to be. But for those who have not been working with your apples, it will be harder to dial up your higher selves in the midst of a heated moment. Yet no matter what the conditions, the choice is yours ... and the choice you make counts and will have a more permanent effect on your relationship than you think. So choose carefully, for counter to what people assume, the kissing-and-making-up afterwards does not really erase a bad choice or its impact. Instead, it goes into your relationship history and serves as a bell that can't ever be fully unrung.

Apologies Work

Whenever an unwanted bell is rung, sincere apologies offer us our only chance of softening its ring. Yet those who have been raised to be competitive consider being wrong an assault to their soul and thus find apologizing very hard to do. Since men in our culture are openly raised to be the best in all areas and at all costs and women are encouraged to more covertly do the same, especially in relationships, the majority of us could be described as competitive. So in the face of our mistakes, there we stand, clearly in error in the eyes of others, while refusing to admit to it or apologize. There is no more foolish way to appear, and this stance serves as a clanging gong that not only can't be unrung, but seems to reverberate even more loudly in the ears of others ... especially our partners. When such a bad choice follows a bad choice, we offer ourselves little hope of recovery.

And so if you want to have continued openness and ongoing communication with your partner and others it's critical that you start soft and stay soft and that rather than react with emotion and challenge, you remain a safe communicator at all times. Once underway, here are some of the things you can do to expand and enhance these communications.

Genuine Safety and Honoring the Information

Once this freer, more open communication begins, it's our job to remain genuinely soft and safe, rather than misuse the information or attack our partner for the truths they are expressing. Thus it's critical that our interest in the material be solely for the purpose of better *understanding* our partner.

Pulling Scarves

When we hear the first parts of our partner's truths expressed more freely under these safer conditions, we can then tug on the pieces of information given by asking questions that bring forth even more of what they are trying to express. These questions are best delivered kindly with the sole purpose of achieving understanding. We can do this most effectively by modeling the interview styles of television hosts such as Larry

King or Charlie Rose, rather than using the gruffer, more confrontational "Crossfire" approach.

To help parents understand how to do this with their children, I use the image of their child holding a magician's top hat filled with variously colored scarves. As their child then dares to show them the tip of one of his or her scarves, the parent's goal is to start with that tip of information to pull out more of the scarf, or the rest of the story. This can also be done with partners and is most effective when done by gently asking sincere, non-judgmental or challenging questions about the tip already exposed, as this creates an environment of safety.

Staying in the Conversation

When someone has found the courage to share their truths with us, it's important that we not sit quietly on the information, as this sends the message that we have dropped out of the communication. In the face of our silence, others will always fill in the blank, so by doing this we not only leave our partner with the need to mind-read but the probable assumption that our withdrawal is due to feelings of disagreement and judgment. Interestingly, many women try to connect through conversation, so they continue to talk, seemingly aimlessly, even when their partner is not responding. As a result of this undirected chatter, their partners become even more bored and silent, and a bad cycle is launched, with each training the other to communicate without connecting.

Expanding Versus Opposing Communications

Many people begin far too early to react to the unfinished fragments of what others are in the beginning stages of expressing. They do this by first interrupting and then arguing for the opposite view of what they thought the other person was planning to say, had they had the opportunity to finish. The person inter-rupted usually interrupts back to attempt to finish what they were originally trying to say or, without even noticing that their point was not heard, strive to defend against the arguments of the other without first clarifying their original viewpoint. Not surprisingly, a debate is underway, often with each person debating the merits of completely different points. Once this amazingly common form of communication is in progress, the experience feels chaotic, as each interrupts the other without first listening to the ideas being presented. When an interrup-tion is accomplished, the person who stole the floor repeats their own argument, free of any influence from the comments of their "opponent," Add to this the flooding of emotion so often felt between partners in conflict, and the most confused and chaotic attempt at communication is underway.

To by-pass this problem, communication experts suggest writing all of the ideas presented onto a flip chart with instruc-tions to the group to remain in an *attitude* of full understander, rather than engage in a debate over any of the ideas presented. Instead everyone is asked to ignore the ideas they don't like, while focusing only on those they do, and then to consider ways to enhance or expand on them whenever possible. This results in each idea being more fully heard with the goal of possibly improving it and then standing without assault, while those that catch the attention of the group are naturally select-ed and further developed.

Processing the Information

Once we have listened to our partner with a gentle ear, a soft heart, and a sincere desire to comprehend, increased under-standing and feelings of real connection tend to follow natu-rally. As a result, the male tendency to want to quickly deliver data and then withdraw from further conversation is not as prominent, nor is the female urge to continue speaking aimlessly for the sake of connection as likely to dominate their communications.

Perception-Checking

If we periodically ask our partner if we are on the same page with them or if they feel heard and understood, we can keep tabs on whether or not we are on point or have wandered off track in our understanding. Yet it's important to be aware that it can be irritating to use the common, yet canned, "I hear you saying (fill in the blank)," so try to reflect what you are understanding in more original and varied ways. It's equally important not to sound like a trained parrot, perfectly feeding back each sentence, since mirroring what someone has just said does not demonstrate understanding and is simply interruptive, rude ... and again irritating.

The best way we know for accomplishing unobtrusive perception-checking is by periodically paraphrasing what we have heard with the sincere goal of seeing if we got it right. Tommy often invites a person to "help me out," particularly when he is getting lost or needs more information. After saying this, he lets them know what he has understood so far and what more he needs in order to get a better grasp of what they are attempting to convey.

Keeping the *Honesty* Apple in the Bowl

When the goal during communication is to be right or win, so common in today's culture, the practice of hiding truths gets woven into the fabric of most of our interactions with each other. It begins with children and is carried forward into business, professional, legal and government practices, as well as in sports and other arenas. As a result of these deep roots of dishonesty in our culture, it has become commonplace, even expected, that we will do what we can to conceal our truths in service of getting our way, winning, making money, or gaining power. This is most commonly reflected in the comment, "That's politics."

But if we want to have successful and bonding communications, starting with our primary partnerships, our *honesty* apples and telling the truth must be returned to the equation. Whenever they are not, this leads to a guaranteed breakdown in communication and brings us to impasse. For anytime we have an invisible hippopotamus hiding under the rug, this unspoken piece will get in the way and block our ability to get clear with each other.

Whenever this happens we must draw on another, more complex skill to return us to a place where we are willing to bring the *honesty* apple and truth back to the table. This skill is called *Clearing*, a technique I developed for those times when our communications get caught in gridlock and cannot be resolved until full honesty is achieved. Whenever all members of a partnership or group want to get beyond an impasse, if they sincerely employ the tools of *Clearing*, they are guaranteed to succeed.

Clearing

Although honesty is claimed as an important value, people don't always tell the truth. It seems this omission of the truth happens as a result of so many of us erroneously assuming we can gloss over our full truths, or even put them aside altogether, in service of some greater cause. Yet if we look deeper into our hearts, there is no cause greater than truth, and anytime one of us fails to disclose the *full* truth it's impossible to achieve clarity. This is most acutely felt in partnership; and we simply can't succeed in having a good one without honesty.

Clearing is a method of clearing up the confused communications that come from our deceptions, whether large or small, and offers us a way to unravel the misunderstandings and problems they create. The reason clearing is able to help us get to clarity is that it is based on participants valuing *honesty* and agreeing to use it without equivocation in its most *pure* form. It is adapted from an ancient Hawaiian practice called Ho'oponopono in which wise elders led people who had come to impasse back to their truth and the clarity that followed. The premise they used to achieve this was that only the truth was honored by the participants, while deceit was highly dishonored. They also recognized that God, who can see into our hearts and knows every nuance of our truths, is always present. Always. And so rather than assume that denying and hiding our truths will get us what we want, they understood that the opposite is true.

Drawing from this concept of valuing honesty during communication I developed a concept called *Clearing,* which is more applicable to small family groups, including couples. During *clearing* the goal is shifted from our commonly used cultural standard of striving to be right to striving to be honest … and it is this shift that allows us to get to clarity, hear and understand each other and to expand our perceptions and wisdom.

Thus in contrast to the dishonesty that has crept into our culture, along with the pervasive yet absurd assumption that God and others won't know our truths if we deny them, all participants in a *clearing* feel obligated to track *all* the nuances of their truths and to openly acknowledge them to their partners and any others attending the *Clearing.* This is successful to the degree the participants are committed to the truth. To accomplish this, group pressure to be honest is established at the outset, and those engaged in *Clearing* tend to conform to this standard.

However, in the privacy of partnership relationships where we lack the benefits of group pressure at the *Clearing,* we need something else to rely on. And this something else lies in our keeping our *Honesty* and *Honoring* apples in our bowl, while being truly honest and honoring from *within* ourselves. If we also add a *Spiritual* apple, this holds us accountable to an even higher standard. In truth, it is best to voluntarily hold ourselves to our own standard of accountability in this way, since in doing so, we are acting as the person we say we want to *be*, outside of any pressure from others, including our partners. Once we learn to do this, our *Honesty* apple is firmly in place and can always be relied on by ourselves and others.

Whenever truth is used by a couple or group who agrees to hold this standard, non-truth stands out like a sore thumb and becomes even more easily visible for all to see. And so the process of declaring the value of the truth at the outset helps the group—or partners—to keep or return their *Honesty* apples to their bowls, and they become newly committed to telling their full truths.

The happy result of setting this precedence is that once everyone's truths are exposed, our partners and others are no longer subjected to denials, defense, excuses and blame and can begin to make sense of the situation. Understanding flows easily out of this atmosphere of honesty, and the group is on their way to renewed levels of clarity and solving their problems.

In addition to honesty, the goal of *Clearing* is to have the first person in the partnership or group who has transgressed against their partner or the others to voluntarily acknowledge this, and they are honored for doing so and disgraced for refusing. Next they are asked to allow the impact of their transgression to penetrate their own awareness and conscience so that they are moved to sincerely feel and express their regrets and to then ask forgiveness. If any of the others are unable to accept this apology, they become the new primary transgressors.

Once this is accomplished, others are asked to share whatever secondary transgressions they have inflicted on their partner or others in reaction to the ones inflicted on them. These might include such things as negative, vengeful and retaliatory thoughts, wishing them ill will or spreading damaging gossip about them.

Sharing transgressions is done until everyone has exposed their most subtle truths and cleared them up with the others. Once this is completed, the truth is out, the air is cleared, forgiveness is given and the participants feel relieved and close again.

WE SAY

Other Forms of Positive Communication

Now that we have presented a crash course in communicating all the way through the rough spots, we have some additional guidelines for keeping communications positive, clear and bonding in your primary partnerships.

Nigglers, Worries, and Highlights

A valued way to maintain closeness is to check in with each other on a daily basis, while being sure to end this check-in time in a way that actively connects you.

To accomplish this, we designed a structure that works well for us and has helped others in our therapy practices and seminars. Some have altered it to better fit their own styles, while others have closely followed our template. The key is to design some way to check in with each other in a friendly safe manner in order to keep things clear between you and to then end on a good note.

This allows you to spend the rest of your day filled with good thoughts about each other and thus associate your partner with positive feelings. It also inspires us to send each other positive energies, which have potent physical and emotional benefits for both the sender and receiver of these thoughts and for the power and synergy of the partnership. And the reverse is also true. Because of this behaviorally reinforcing component, we do this at least once a day, or anytime we sense something has come between us—even if it's small. In this way we are able to keep the energy between us clear and loving on a regular basis, rather than allow hours or days of negative thoughts and emotion to build up a head of steam and damage our feelings for each other—the stuff that growing apart is made of. Here's the technique.

We check in at least once a day in order to ask if either of us has any "nigglers" or "sweater-snaggers" that have caught our attention and don't feel clear. This gives both of us an opportunity to share things like feeling hurt or disdained or in some other way "snagged" when our partner has done something such as ignoring us, speaking to us in harsh tones or failing to include us in an activity or a decision affecting both of us.

It's critical that these *nigglers* or *snaggers* are conveyed gently and in a *Side-By-Side* manner with the goal of having both partners feel clearer and closer, rather than using them as a way to simply complain, scold or punish. It's also important to guard against creating any feeling between you that talking about nigglers will be uncomfortable or even dreaded—and thus ultimately avoided. Nor do you want them to become a substitute for the unpleasant "We need to Talk" conversations that are so common between couples. Instead, you want to be sure that these daily discussions will reduce, rather than expand any misunderstandings and tension between you. To achieve this, it's essential that these conversations are held while clearly keeping *all* of your apples in your bowl.

It's equally important that the partner being told of the niggler remain open and interested in the content and what can be learned from it and improved, rather than quickly shut down and bat the information away by defending and arguing that it is not true. Many men and a good deal of women feel that all conversations that might have the content of a *niggler* must be avoided at all costs. Yet this is an attitude that will give them more of the very problems they are hoping to avoid.

Anytime such a defensive approach to sharing information gets activated, the communication immediately breaks down. At this juncture, whatever information was intended to be conveyed has been derailed and the subject shifts to the denials and defense of the partner terrified of hearing anything not perceived as positive. This kind of fear of hearing anything that is not viewed as highly positive lies at the heart of communication problems between couples and serves as a bigger threat than most realize to their continuing closeness.

Ironically, the resistance of the person who does not want to engage in these kinds of communications is based on their fear that some weakness or error might be exposed. This is further fueled by an erroneous assumption that we should not have any weaknesses or make errors and that if we do, something has gone wrong. Thus, rather than easily face and acknowledge these, quickly learn from them, apologize if appropriate and move on, the resistance to taking these steps serves as an enormous barrier to going forward. So rather than get the niggler on the table and easily handled in proportion to its impact on the relationship, a much larger problem—the resistance—must now be addressed. And because of the nature of resistance, this usually ends in impasse and cannot be cleared.

Unfortunately, the inability of a couple to get beyond their small nigglers results in increasing feelings of alienation between them, and the wonderful feelings they initially associated to their partner are no longer positive, but now become tainted and eventually negative.

On the other hand, if the conversation is allowed, heard and acknowledged, the partner first bringing up the niggler feels heard, understood and cared about. And the result is an expanded understanding between them, and feelings of closeness are not only returned but increased.

Although both men and women can get defensive, men are known for having a harder time staying open to feedback they perceive as "negative" or critical in some way. As a result of this hypersensitivity to feedback, they can often get defensive, even when the comment is not in fact critical of them. This bristling ironically creates increased distance between the couple as well as the criticism he was hoping to avoid.

Whenever this happens, distance, rather than closeness between them has not only been created, they are now both afraid to have these conversations about nigglers that are so important to keeping feelings between them clear and connecting.

To counter this communication quagmire, once a niggler is gently presented, it's critical that the person receiving the information do their best to be the *Understander*. This is best done by keeping all of your apples and communication skills in place while listening in accordance with the guidelines for being an *Understander*. It's equally important that if a niggler is not quickly cleared, that time is set aside to get all the way through it.

As tempting as it might be to avoid the problems that talking about nigglers might create, it's critical that couples understand that if nigglers are left unspoken, they become one of the most potent dangers to the survival of the relationship. Here's why. Unspoken irritants or ones that are denied and can't get cleared do not go away as we had hoped. Instead they are repeatedly visualized and reviewed as they gather a negative storm in the privacy of our minds which we then direct at our partners. Although many men also do this, women are particularly prone to it. And once this pattern begins, our partners can feel the negative energy coming at them and usually return the favor. And so a tit-for-tat battle of harmful energy is exchanged in silence, while we invisibly, yet steadily grow apart. Because of this dangerously negative effect on our love and partnership of not discharging our nigglers, the value of doing so becomes even clearer.

Once all the nigglers are cleared, we then ask each other if either has any "worries" or other conversations we would like to discuss on such topics as concerns about money, the children, family, work, health and so on that might affect the relationship. This sets aside a regular opportunity to talk about important subjects and to bond and feel closer in the process of understanding and resolving them.

Finally, when the nigglers and worries have been handled, we ask if either of us has any "highlights." This gives both of us an opportunity to scan our day for the times when we were delighted by something the other did or when we felt particularly in love, valued and close. Sharing and hearing these highlights not only reminds us of our special moments together, but reinforces both of us for having created these good times and positive associations toward each other—including such things as phone calls, emails, special food purchases, small gifts, sharing high points and other parts of our day, suggesting plans for the weekend or an evening "date," offers of help, cards, love notes and so on. It highlights in our own minds the good points of our partner and reflects them back in a way that makes them feel seen and understood as well as cherished and honored.

These exercises have been designed with a very powerful behavioral component of putting each of us into a positive frame of mind toward the other throughout each day. By doing this at least once daily before going off on your day, you are each given an opportunity to discharge and clear anything that might otherwise leave you with bad thoughts and feelings or negative associations linked to your partner. Following this, both partners are then encouraged to continue to scan for the good things between them, which helps them to focus on positive associations toward each other throughout the day.

Life on Our Toes

Other ways we can keep our partnerships positive is to remember to be as loving and playful with each other following commitment as we did during courtship. For example most of us during courtship were excited about seeing each other, liked to "hang out" together, to flirt and play and were consistently enthusiastic about the interests and activities of our partner. In short, we were in the relationship on our toes with a sense of positive enthusiasm, playfulness and being ready to go. Yet following commitment, many people put their heels down and begin to resist the interests and activities of their partner, begrudge the time it takes to hang out together and stop being enthusiastic about the interests and activities of their partner. In short, their partner has clearly lost their place of importance to them and this serves as a daily hurt that eats away at the bonds between them. So if who you are is a person genuinely in love with your partner and want to continue in a close and loving relationship with them, it's critical that you understand the importance of keeping your heels up in all of your interactions with them.

We Versus Me

A big idea Tom brings to the success of good partnership is the importance of conducting it from the point of view of "we" versus "me." By one partner focusing their life on themselves or following the *me* route, they return to their singles life activities once the courtship is over, while their partner is trying to continue with the *we* experience they were enjoying during courtship. The idea comes out of some research he and a colleague conducted on how men tend to commit to staying married—while acting single—rather than making their relationship a wonderful experience as women are more prone to do. Yet partners who want to feel truly bonded, enjoy the synergy that true closeness creates, and remain outrageously in love must understand that this is more likely to happen if they conduct their relationship as a *we* versus *me* experience.

The Connecting Power of Touch

Contact, both physical and visual, offers partners a valuable and connecting form of communication. When touch is ample in our primary partnerships, the bonding or cuddle hormone called Oxytocin is released, and we feel closer, more attracted and more secure in the relationship.

Because physical touch and extended eye contact make up such a large part of most courtships, this connection is usually strong during that early phase of our relationships. However in cases where both physical touch and visual gazing drop off following courtship, their absence has the reverse effect. Thus it's important for couples wanting to continue to feel close, or recapture closeness once lost, to be aware of the power of physical touch and visual stimulation in supporting their connection and to resume things like looking at each other, holding hands, kissing, caressing and offering foot, head and back massages. Similarly, when these energies are sent to others outside the relationship, whether casually, during fantasies, or in reality, it has a weakening effect on the bonds and feelings of connection between the couple.

Sex

Both men and women often drop out of their sexual relationship for a variety of reasons. Women may give in to inertia without realizing that inertia is as much a killer in this arena as it is in others. Men may assume sex should always be like it was in their 20s and fail to adjust to the changes of maturity. Both may drop out due to all of the sticks that have come between them. Or they might dilute their interest in each other by looking at others they have no negative history with or find attractive at first blush, thus allowing their *commitment, honoring* and *honesty* apples to roll out of their bowls.

Whatever the reason, dropping out causes a serious disconnection in the positive feelings that flow between them, including the powerful sexual feelings that used to be directed only at each other on a more frequent basis. So if any of this is happening, understand the seriousness of the threat it poses to the partnership and make choices accordingly.

Good Boy, Wally!

With all these tools in place to help us navigate through the hard and happy parts of communication, it's important to remember the *real* purpose of these interactions.

We have a very sharp and playful friend in her 80s who also happens to be a woman of considerable wealth. Her assistant shared with us one day that she had hung most of our friend's Armani suits on a clothes rack in preparation for a trip. Then, to her horror, as the assistant was returning to the bedroom to pack the suits, she arrived in time to see our friend's dog lift his leg and carefully aim at the Armanis. It was clear that he didn't want his mistress to travel, and they both watched as he carefully sprayed the outfits on the rack. The assistant stood paralyzed, not knowing what to do, when our friend broke the silence with her delightful laugh and in a throaty voice declared, "Good boy, Wally!"

Tom often says he would *love* to come back as one of our friend's dogs, but the real truth is we *all* want to be as thoroughly understood and loved for who we are, bad habits and all, as Wally. Yet in truth it is even more special to be the one to give this gift of complete understanding and unrestricted love that our friend offers Wally and the rest of her dogs. Once we know how to do this, everything else falls into place, since this is the real goal of all our interactions with our partners and others … and is the true purpose of our lives.

"If we do not change our daily lives we cannot change the world."

—THICH NHAT HANH

NINE

So, Now What?

*"The power of man has grown in every sphere,
except over himself."*
—WINSTON CHURCHILL

WE SAY

We were going to make certain that this relationship would last and wanted to be certain of the outcome before we committed to the process of partnership. Looking back on the early start of this search for interpersonal certainty, it seems that we were just plain naïve. And we thank God!

We believe that it was that naiveté that allowed us to think in terms that ran so counter to our culture and the expectations of others that we were inspired by our optimism to come up with a completely new approach. Really, who were we to think that with failed relationships behind us, the toots in front of us and friends chanting the enjoy-it-because-it-won't-last mantra, that we could possibly do anything that would insure a positive outcome; that the relationship would not only go the distance, but would do so in fine style, continuing to expand in a seemingly limitless fashion. But that is what is happening.

And as the relationship has expanded beyond our original dreams, we have also come to realize how unique it is and how fortunate we were to have had the histories that mandated we do nothing less than *settle for more* if we were going to sink ourselves into another significant relationship. It became clear that our past relationship experiences had served us well, and that without them we would be lump-along candidates ... and that because of them we would not. And it is those experiences that have produced the material in this book.

Moreover what we have found through our relationship coaching and counseling of couples and individuals is that what we have developed is powerful enough to enable us to help people achieve partnership success, rather than help them mop up their failures. The good news is we *can* front load this process.

Some erroneously assume we are able to benefit from our Model due to our experience. They say such things as, "You two are older and have the advantage of silver hair wisdom. But what about those of us who are younger and less experienced and lack the wisdom you possess?"

Here's our answer: If we were to tell you that you can avoid losing several digits by not putting your hand in the Cuisinart while it is running, would you feel you had to first experience the whirring blades slicing several inches off your fingers before you could refrain from plunging your fist into the Cuisinart bowl? After seeing others pulling out bloody stumps, would you still say you needed to experience it for yourselves?

Relationships are no different. We don't need to suffer the agony and unkindness, the defensiveness and distancing that go with relationship failures. People who truly want to be in a relationship of unlimited possibilities can do so *without having to fail first in order to succeed. This is the promise we offer!*

Instead you can go directly to success if you will simply raise the bar on the standard you want to hold for your partnership;

then continue with the courtship behaviors that brought you so much happiness when you first met; and finally select and live by the apples you value, starting with embodying their qualities and then living by them on a daily basis.

By using this simple formula, you not only *settle for more*, but reap unique levels of unlimited, outrageous and joyful partnership. It's simpler, not harder, to engage in this course than any other course you have tried. You have only to leave the starter's gate and begin, even if you are the first one out. And if you begin, you will get there.

So what now? This is a leap, but imagine if you will a family or a neighborhood or a community, a town, city, a state or a country or a group of countries ... where everyone is able to create a relationship that works ... where everyone has a clear picture of the relationship they want to be in and are taking responsibility for bringing it about.

Most certainly doable. Then why don't we do it?

The answer lies in *YOUR* relationship. Yes, YOUR relationship. And that is where it has to start ... and conversely, that is where it will all end. So what do we mean? Why are we resting the hope of the world on your relationship? This is not a burden, as it might seem at first, but is simple and, as we said, doable. This is why and how it works.

We can't expect that neighbors, counties, states or countries can get their relationships with each other to work if we can't even make our own relationships work. If we can't get it together in our own living rooms, by clearly defining and living by our apples, then why would we expect it to happen in a larger universe made up of individuals just like us? It won't if we don't. It will if we will.

Ridiculously simple!

Yes, we know all about the "yeah buts" that surface when big goals are suggested, and we have heard them all. Yeah, but what about the people who won't do it if I do? Yeah, but what about the people who just want to win or the people who don't care if it works or not, or the sociopaths, or the crooks and thugs or the ——, or the——or the——? Well, what about them? What do they really have to do with me developing, defining and living by my apples in the context of the relationship in which I want to be with the partner of my choice?

And why can't we expand that out and have our behavior with *everyone* consistent with our apples ... and by doing so *always* be in the best relationships possible, if that is what we want? Because just as in our primary relationship, the minute we remove one of the apples from our bowl, we are no longer in the relationships we want, no matter what others might do. That is as true in our relationships with the supermarket checker, the gas station attendant, pastor, priest, rabbi, cleric, police person, bank teller, mayor, movie star, *everyone,* as it is with our partner.

Coming from this point of view, the jig's up because we can now see the choice is ours and that we have two choices: either continue to adapt to the lowering-of-the-bar and *settling for less* or raise the bar on all of our relationships and be willing only to *settle for more.*

If you choose the former, no harm no foul. It is your relationship and your choice. But now you can make it consciously. At the least, you will know why it is going south and you will have new tools available to change the direction if that is what you want.

If you choose the latter, your relationships will never be the same. You will continually have the opportunity to experience the power generated by declaring how you are going to be in relationships and then being that person and standing for what you have declared. Once actively in this mode, you will begin to see that it is not limited to just your primary partnerships, but that it works and is applicable in *all* relationships.

But there is one more kicker here, and it's even bigger than what happens in the relationship you conduct in your own life and living room. Here's why ...

the shape of your relationship shapes your world

... and this offers a solution to the conundrum posited by Sir Winston above. We **DO** have control and thus power over ourselves in relationships. And this gives us control and power over the shape of *our* world.

A story from Tom's youth demonstrates how this works:

It was early in my first marriage. We were living in the San Francisco Bay area and going to dinner at the home of a couple, we'll call them Bob and Janet, both of whom I had known since childhood. Still in our mid 20s, I had only recently married while they were "old hands" at this business, well into their sixth year. They had also been high school sweethearts, so they had a familiarity with each other that gave them the appearance of knowing what they were doing. Shortly after arriving at their home it became apparent Bob was in the midst of some sort of issue with Janet and the sticks were flying, subtly at first but eventually turning to outright nastiness. He was curt, belittling, dishonoring, sarcastic, argumentative and determined to be right.

I remember little of the evening other than how unpleasant it was. The mood, the energy, were so negative that it was palpable, affecting my outlook and mood, and permanently altering my perception of my long term friend. I didn't realize it at the time, but that seminal evening was the source of an argument that I initiated on the way home, one in which I am certain I was most unpleasant. It was the kind of argument that left permanent negative feelings in the heart of my ex-wife and shaped her view of who I was. More than that, I left the evening with a picture of Bob that remains with me to this day.

And I am but one of thousands who have come into contact with Bob and Janet over the lifetime of their relationship. Imagine what their Relationship Effect Diagram might look like if my evening with them was typical of their interpersonal interaction. Their stick behaviors would send ripples into the environment affecting all those around them who would in due time affect others, who would in turn affect others *ad nauseum.*

I have clear recollections of times when my own behaviors have served the function of the proverbial stone thrown far out into still waters, causing ripples eventually covering the entire surface of the lake as they lap back to the edges of the shore. You can begin to see that the effect and impact on the social environment will increase exponentially as it spreads out from the original behavior.

This can be both a problem and an opportunity. For if our negative behaviors, those things we do that limit and ultimately destroy the relationship, can send negative ripples into the social environment with untoward though unintended consequences, then why can't the obverse be true? Why couldn't positive relationship behaviors, those that are respectful, loving, kind and supportive, positively impact the social environment?

You might be thinking, this is nice theory, but how can what I do affect the environment simply by having someone observe my behavior? We don't know the exact mechanism, but the phenomenon has been demonstrated repeatedly.

Studies show us that when we do something nice to someone, they feel good. This seems fairly obvious, and people report it to be true. We also know it because in controlled environments afforded by clinical studies, we can take an individual's blood levels before and after someone has done something nice to or for them. And what we find is that Serotonin, the neurotransmitter that makes us feel good, is released and found elevated in the blood samples of those who have had something nice done to or for them.

But here is the important part: When people simply observe something nice being done to someone else, *they* also feel good and *their* Serotonin levels are elevated as well. So, here is the inescapable conclusion: The way you are with your partner has an effect on those who observe you. When you are being a twerp, it affects others negatively, who in turn affect others negatively, and so on. And when you are being nice, it makes people feel good, and they in turn will make others feel good ... and so on.

So let's fantasize for a moment. Imagine what it would be like if you had grown up in an environment in which this perspective was the norm and the behaviors consistent with it were expected. What would you and the world be like if, from the moment of your birth, all you had ever known and seen were people making their relationships the number one priority in their lives? And they expected the same from you. What kind of a world would we experience and how hard would it be to live and survive in such a world?

And why didn't we grow up in a world like this? Given that we spend the majority of the time in our developmental years learning within a formalized school structure, why don't these schools integrate a relationship-development curriculum into the culture of the school? From the day a child enters the school system, why aren't they taught both formally and informally that there is nothing more important in the world than our relationships? Why don't schools immerse their faculty in relationship training, requiring that they model apple-based behaviors as well as work with the children constantly in this domain? And why don't they require that parents participate in relationship-support training so that their children have a relationship-friendly environment at home, where what they are learning at school is practiced by their families? Why don't we immerse our children in an educational system that is seamless in its relationship imperative, where all children are included and all learn the value and power of creating a world based on relationships that work? Why have we settled for less?

This is fantasy, you say, and that is why it can't happen! You say you would never be able to create an educational system of this caliber because you couldn't get parents off the dime or school faculty or administration or unions to support it. Just as in the yeah-buts, we have heard all the reasons why an educational system that places a premium on the children's ability to be successful in their relationships just won't work. But here's the deal. It does work. It has worked.

Bobbie is a co-founder of a school in Hawaii where the children's interactions with others *is* the curriculum. And because the gentle kindness they learned to so abundantly express to others was observed by all who met them, the children had the same far-reaching impact on others that we described earlier. This is not the place, nor is there room, to describe this school in detail. Suffice it to say that not only did the children excel intellectually but socially, and that the long-term effects on their family structures and the Honolulu community, while not as easily studied, anecdotally were remarkable.

The children from that original class are grown and many have their children in this school. They are well equipped to operate in the world, while remaining squarely planted in their apples. Moreover, children in Australia attending a school using this same approach have, over the past ten years, been consistently placed in gifted programs the following year.

So, we know that it works ... and that it works easily and well with far-reaching positive effects. So why are we *settling for less* for so many of our children and our children's children?

For that matter why are we *settling for less* for anyone, anywhere? Why do we settle for less in so many settings ... from those we work with, or those who work for us or for whom we work? Why do we let the apples slide in these relationships and allow people to bumble about the world blatantly interacting with us in ways that are clearly inconsistent with the apples we have chosen for our relationships ... and in dealing with them why do we temporarily take certain apples out of our own bowl? You do it, and we do it. But now that we know about the importance of the apples and are committed to keeping them in our bowl and running our relationships and lives based on them, we do it much less frequently. And when we know we are doing it, we clean it up. Using the "doings" presented in chapter 8, we find we are able to be the people we want to be in the relationships we desire much more of the time.

So, we've come to the end of this conversation that began a couple of hundred pages ago. And now let us tell you why we *really* want to be in the relationship we have described in this book.

We are terribly disappointed with the condition of our world. The level of congressional and political sniping and hostility has reached an historical high and shows no signs of abating; the compassion this country shows for the least, the lost and the forgotten is deplorable; our understanding of how to use our country's incredible resources to lead the world successfully is demonstrably deficient; human life is viewed by many in the world as disposable; wars between regions and countries are ongoing, with no intention on the part of the warring parties to cease their activities. As far as relationships go, the state of the world reflects major failures. But here is the point.

Why would we expect people, countries or the world for that matter to get along if we are unable to make our own relationship work? Or another way of putting it is, until we can make our relationship work, the world will be in a state of ooots and toots.

But we could change this faster than we think if we were each willing to get out of the starter's gate and be the first to begin doing it differently, starting in our own living rooms with our partners. For if we are willing, and you are each willing, things could change overnight.

We dream of the day that world leaders will declare their desire and intention to be in a relationship with the rest of the world in a manner that is based on clearly defined and articulated apples, and that we would be able to count on their behavior reflecting that declaration.

But we know it will never happen if we are unable to do the same in our relationships at home. Why would we expect them to do something that is far more intricate than something we are unable or unwilling to do? We can't, and they won't. If we can, they can. We know we can. We know you can if that is your desire. And why wouldn't that be your desire?

Yup. We are back to the question we asked at the beginning of the book. Why would anyone *settle for less?* We know why they do. But once they become aware that they can change the world by changing their relationships, no answer suffices. As for us:

We have committed ourselves to *Settle for More.*

"The shape of your relationship shapes the world."
—TOM MERRILL

EPILOGUE

Recovering Our Innocence

"Babies are such a nice way to start people."
—Don Herold

We had put the finishing touches on the book you are holding in your hands and were preparing to deliver it to our New York publisher when Bobbie broke her leg. We did not want to navigate New York on crutches, so we postponed the trip for a month.

Hailey, our six-year-old granddaughter who has a direct avenue to our hearts, heard about the calamity. Several days later we found a hand delivered, somewhat mussed envelope in the mailbox addressed to Grandma Bobbie. Inside, was a note as carefully wrapped as a six-year-old can manage with a beautiful portrait of grandma accompanied by a heartfelt message, "I hope you Feell Beter BoBy, Love Hailey." Tucked inside the note was a crumpled dollar bill folded over and flattened as if it had been freshly extricated from a piggy bank.

Checking to make sure that mom knew Hailey was sending out money, we called and were assured that yes, Hailey had cleared the decision to send a dollar from her piggy bank so that Bobbie could buy something to make her feel better. Bobbie did feel better and mended quickly. And Hailey's good wishes helped. But the dollar was not spent. Instead it hangs framed in our office as a constant reminder of the innocence, the kindness, and the possibilities that children unabashedly offer in their relationships with others.

Fast Forward.

So now we live in the world of adults where we have been told to put away such childish things—and have learned this lesson all too well. What happened between the innocence, kindness and caring of the "Hailey period" and the "grown up" world of relationships, where one out of two marriages end in divorce and non-marital primary relationships are in constant danger of extinction?

Our inability to first develop and then remain positively engaged emotionally in primary relationships reflects a major failing in the world. Whatever it is that we put away when we became adults, we need back—not as children, but as mature adults.

And it is this magical and powerful ability to *be* truly loving, open, innocent and kind at the core of ourselves that we bring to the human experience as children and then lose in the course of becoming adults in our culture that we want back.

The good news is that if you will now follow the Model you have learned about in this book, you can transform your relationship to one that includes the kind of unlimited possibilities seen in the "Hailey period." Based on our results with clients and in seminars, we submit that you *can Settle for More.* And that's the promise we offer. Guaranteed.

"Settle for More."

—*TOM AND BOBBIE MERRILL*

How Does It Work
in the Real World?

*"In a time of drastic change it is the learners
who inherit the future. The learned usually find
themselves equipped to live in a world that
no longer exists."* —ERIC HOFFER

From the moment we began to share our Model with others
in therapy and in workshops we were asked to explain how it
might be applied in a variety of specific situations. The dialogue
generated from these questions was wonderful and made a great
contribution to understanding how the Model works in real life.

We felt the question and answer format was an ideal way to
get some great relationship information to the larger public
audience and so began to write a weekly Tom-says-Bobbie-says
column called, *Solving the Relationship Puzzle*. The column was
picked up by the Cox News/New York Times group to be sent
nationally to 600 newspapers using their service and is seen
weekly in papers from South America to Massachusetts.

We have included a small sampling of the columns in the
following pages that are representative of the questions we are
asked, touching on the concerns that most of us have. Our
hope is that our responses will achieve the same result experienced in our seminars, workshops and individual sessions;

that is, a greater understanding of how the Model works in real life.

We invite you to read our weekly column. If it is not running in your local newspaper, you can find the current columns online at the Atlanta Journal Constitution Webpage www.AJC.com or both the current and past columns at www.TomMerrill.com. We hope you find them both enjoyable and helpful in your *Settling For More* journey.

⁂

SOLVING THE RELATIONSHIP PUZZLE
The Art of Unlimited Relationships
Nationally Published Weekly Column

● What's the Rule?

Dear Bobbie and Tom,

I want to know how to play fair. My partner will do something mean and then when I respond with a similar behavior, he complains. How can we develop rules so that we treat each other fairly?

Bobbie says: Whenever we fall in love, we put the best we have to offer on the table and hope it will be enough to win the heart of the person we love. Because neither party holds anything back during this early stage of a relationship, a concern about fairness rarely surfaces.

Yet this worry often arises later as a result of our failure to be as generous once we feel confident the person we love also loves us. At this juncture we naively start to hold back the very things that won their love as we worry that we might be giving more than we are getting. So instead of continuing to give all we've got we now carefully watch the "scales of equal measure" to make sure we are getting our fair share.

We begin to think and say things like, "I'll rub your neck if you rub mine." Or, "I don't want to go to your movie because you didn't go to mine." We also withdraw listening when we don't feel listened to, yell if we get yelled at, and want to hurt if we have been hurt.

This holding back replaces our initial generosity and kindness with a sense of contraction, jealousy, competition and argument. This takes us off the track of giving all we've got in the spirit of generating *more* in our lives and puts us on a stingy path filled with constrictions and squabbles over not getting enough.

To reverse this trend that invariably leads to friction, we must remember that love is seeded in a generosity of kindness and will die if kindness is no longer active and ample.

I have found that the only way to get out of this "tit" for "tat" arrangement is to give as much as I can, regardless of how my partner is behaving. By doing this I take my own pettiness off the table and stick with being the person I want to be. If my partner continues on the "tit" for "tat" course, in time it will become apparent that I have picked the wrong person.

But if I am steady about being a kind and giving person, and he decides to do the same, then we both act with the generosity of kindness we used during our courtship and are blessed by an abundance of kindness in our partnership and home.

Tom says: Rules are great and necessary in games. But relationships are not a game. There is no such thing as a winner or loser in relationships that have gone beyond "just good enough" to something truly special. So, the first thing is to get out of the game business with your partner and into the relationship business.

You will still need to agree with your partner on how to conduct yourselves in the complexities of interacting, but the only rules would be your rules on how you behave and your partner's rules on how he or she behaves.

And that makes it very simple, because there is only one rule you need to follow, and that is, "be nice." Any other rules you feel are necessary will be to accommodate each other when you are not being nice.

What we have observed is that as a culture we set the bar too low on our expectations of and demands for ourselves in relationships while setting the bar higher for our partner. We excuse our "just good enough" behavior by saying, "well you did——" fill in the blank.

If you really stop to think about it, why would you do anything to or with the person you love that wasn't based on being nice? We have excuses for why we feel justified in using unkind behavior, but they are just that. Excuses. And those excuses are the genesis of relationships that are "just good enough to stay in," or "not bad enough to leave."

If you or your partner need help being nice, then get help. When both partners play by the "be nice" rule, the relationship will move from 'just good enough' to one that is as good as it can be, and you are on your way to a relationship of unlimited possibilities.

◕ Why Settle for More? Or Going Along to Get Along?

Dear Bobbie and Tom,

I have read your columns and notice your constant refrain to "settle for more," rather than "lower the bar" on our relationship expectations. I have always heard you should "go along to get along" which seems to contradict your advice. I am in a 2-year committed relationship, and we are following the go-along model and get along pretty well. We have fights like everyone else and if things get testy we take a break from each other. Like all relationships ours could be better. But why should I raise the subject with him and risk getting in a fight over what I want? Even worse, what if he likes the bar where it is and says if I don't like it I can take a hike? Why should I insist on settling for more if it means I may end up with *nothing* to settle for?

Tom says: There is no "should" implied here. However, the relationship you have described and identify as being "like everyone else" does sound a lot like those we see in our office. And most who come to see us professionally are not doing so to report on how successful they are in their relationships— rather, they are looking for ways to improve a troubled partnership. So, I would want to know a little bit more about what you are willing to settle for and why. AND I would like to know the same of your partner.

There is a lot to be said for the "going along" way of directing your future. It is an easy way to avoid discomfort in the short run. Day by day it doesn't make much difference in the direction of your relationship. However, we have heard from many who have looked back after years of "going along" and have found that it has gotten them to a place far different than they had wanted and hoped for.

What are the causes of the fights and testiness? How could things be better? Why would your stating what you want in a relationship cause a fight? If the answers to these and other probing questions I or any other therapist would ask is that the relationship is not one that is honoring, honest, supportive caring and loving (to list just a few of the characteristics that are found in truly wonderful relationships), then you have settled for less. And that is ok if you are doing it out of choice. Just know there is a cost involved in lowering the bar that should be factored in when you are making your decision. If "going along" is simply a euphemism for giving up what is important to you in order to avoid a fight, then the cost is horrendous. Only you can decide if it is worth it.

Bobbie says: Like Tom, I too want to ask some questions about why you would consider living your precious life with even a slightly lowered bar, or if you understand that by doing so you risk destroying the very relationship you are trying to protect.

Perhaps the key question is, "Are you truly 'going along' in service of 'getting along' or in hopes of preserving the relationship at great cost to yourself?" Your concern about upsetting your partner or losing him if you discuss your preferences implies that you would rather be compliant than risk challenge and loss. If so, be aware that anytime we accept such terms, as women—as well as many men—often do, we lower the bar on the kind of relationship we are willing to have. This is a defining moment for the relationship and our lives as it sets our standard below all possibility for true happiness. Here's why.

Although it seems at this early juncture as though you are taking only a small dip into a lower standard, this establishes a trend, and over time you will likely accommodate to less and less. What the women and men who do this fail to understand is that their decision to settle for less is rarely genuine and does not really sit well with them. As a result they spend many hours in the privacy of their minds or with friends, nursing dangerous feelings toward their partners and relationships. This common, yet destructive pastime drives the bar and their feelings even lower, and in time they no longer feel in love or seek spending much time together. Many will stay in the relationship at this point for the sake of security, but begin the process of living their lives separately. Others have had enough of an eroding relationship and to their partner's surprise, leave, often abruptly. So the decision to "go along to get along" can be more dangerous than it first appears, often setting a course for the ultimate demise of the relationship.

Although, as Tom says, no "should" is implied here, our goal is to make you and others more aware of the path the "go along" course takes, so that if you choose it, you and your partner will do so more consciously. We also hope that with more information, you might both consider *settling for more.*

Is It the Man?

Dear Bobbie and Tom,

I really enjoy reading your column. Although you focus on different points, overall you seem to agree on everything, and it sounds as if you two have an ideal relationship. I truly believe that I could have the same kind of relationship if I had the right man. Bobbie, you keep saying how good a partner Tom is, and by the way he talks about how to treat a woman ... who couldn't have a good relationship with him?

Tom says: Your question gives us the opportunity to address an issue that seems to keep coming up in our workshops and seminars. And that is the idea that if someone has the right partner, other than the one they now have, they can make the relationship work. This way of thinking is great in fairy tails but not so functional in real life. And here's why. Thinking that there is a prince somewhere who will pull you out of the everyday relationship you are in comes from the belief that your partner, not you, is responsible for the health of your relationship. Thoughts like, "If only my partner would do things right —say nice things, cook dinner, wash the dog, take me to the movies," and so on.

If your partner was never like this and has no desire to be, chances are he will never reach prince status. Or, if he looked like royalty when you first connected but has "changed" over time, then you're saying you could have had the relationship you wanted if your partner had not changed.

Whatever the reason, even if he is a jerk, you do not get to put the responsibility for the failure on his side of the bed. Take a deep breath, own up to your part in choosing him and figure our whether you want to leave or stay. If you choose option two, the only thing you can do is work on your contribution to the relationship misery, and happiness.

If he started out as your prince and now hops and has warts, then you know at the least he has the potential to regain his crown. But you cannot do this by yourself. You need to engage him in a partnership experience of repairing your partnership. But be ready ... he may say you went from princess to Broomhilda. This is the case in the greatest percentage of couples that we see in therapy and our seminars. Each partner sees the other as the one that has changed, and it would all have worked out if they had not.

Bobbie is a wonderful person to be in a relationship with. She wants to make it work. If she did not, I would not be married to her. If I didn't, she would not want to be married to me. The fact that she does so makes it very easy for me to do everything I can to insure that the relationship does nothing but get better. So, you see, it is not a matter of having the right partner, it is a matter of having the right partnership, and *your* willingness to make it so.

Bobbie says: This is a big question that women often ask. The answer is complex so I will address it here and again in future columns. Note that you mention how often I describe Tom as a wonderful partner. I do and that is because he truly is. But what you have not seemed to notice is that he also describes me as a wonderful partner. And it is this gift of being good partners to each other that makes our relationship work. But you are not the first woman who has overlooked that good partnering is a contribution we *both* make to our partnership, so the question is why?

Why do women so often assume that if only they had the "ideal" man that their partnerships would automatically work? Why is it they fail to more deeply consider what their contribution to the problems might be and how completely new and different kinds of contributions to partnership from the culturally accepted ones currently used could turn a difficult relationship into a wonderful one? What if, rather than assume they are *already* doing everything right, as I initially did, more women strived to unearth what new things they might bring to the relationship table to better enhance their partnership possibilities? This is what I ultimately did after realizing that women, too, can do better, and the results are quite different from the standard way women often show up in relationships.

For example, although many women yearn to replicate Cinderella's "ideal" relationship primarily by being beautiful enough to land the "prince," we are not told what happened after their night of dancing at the ball and thus have no model for what comes after courtship.

We know only that they lived "happily ever after," but we are not shown how they did it. Did Cinderella take up acting like her envious stepmother, her bullying stepsisters or her kind fairy godmother? Did she rely solely on her beauty to inspire the Prince to continue his chivalrous behavior? And if he slipped, did she become a disappointed and self-appointed "corrector" or begin her search for a new prince? In short, did Cinderella alter her view of the Prince as perfect and default to scanning for signs of warts and hopping about? Or did she hold steady to looking for the good in him and continue to love and honor him, even when his crown slipped from time to time?

All of these feminine prototypes fill our world, and men, equally armed with an array of styles, tend to respond in accordance to whichever one shows up. It's hard to tell who sets off the "tit" for "tatting" reactions to each other, but the primary argument tends to boil down to who is the blue blood and who is the toad.

So the question is: do you really need a prince to make your relationship wonderful or do you yourself need to be better? To address this question, I suggest women more sincerely consider exactly what it is they bring to the table, consciously choose to be the best they can be, and if it's still not working, then, and only then, will they really know if they are with the wrong partner.

● Do You Do It?

Dear Tom and Bobbie,

I have gotten hooked on your column, but my husband hates that I keep holding your standard for good partnership up to him. He's also been able to catch me more than a few times in not holding to the standard myself. Both of you seem happy to do what it takes to raise the bar and ask more of yourselves. My husband questions whether or not you can really do it.

Bobbie says: Yes we can and do. And this surprises us as much as it may surprise you and others, including your husband. Yet once we made the decision to raise the bar on our concept of what partnership can be, the act of treating each other in a loving and honoring way not only followed naturally and easily for us, but has been highly rewarding.

Even more surprising is that once we got started on this new way of being, we both became addicted to filling our own hearts and home with this more pleasant and joyful energy. In fact it is our attachment to feeling loving from within as well as closer to each other that prompts us to each self-correct whenever we have strayed from this goal, rather than wait for the other to catch and coax us back into line. It seems as though once we established our new standard, falling below it feels instantly uncomfortable and we are anxious to get back to being the kind of person and partner we have declared we want to be.

An unexpected benefit of this is that in addition to the good feelings it generates within ourselves and for each other, new research reveals that watching people be kind to others has a positive effect on those watching us interact this way. This is due to the mood-elevating hormones such as serotonin that are secreted within people watching kind interactions between others.

And so not only does our higher standard of interaction make us feel better while enhancing our partnership, it enables our children, other family members and friends to feel happier and more positive in our presence. This is a very powerful way for partners to strengthen themselves and their families as well as to have a positive impact on the world around them. If we think of the implications of this, we can begin to see that simply by raising our own personal standard for interactions between partners we can have a far-reaching and powerful impact on the betterment of the world.

Thus if we can begin to get over the idea that treating our partners as well as we did during courtship is too hard to do, we would each be more willing to begin. We would also discover in the process that treating others consistently well is not as difficult as we have made it out to be. And the ripple effect could turn our world into a far kinder, more loving experience as each partnership takes up the mantle.

And so back to your question—given these possibilities, why would any of us want to do it any other way? And why would we so doggedly assume that being loving and kind in our primary relationships will be harder than the alternative? What do we get out of sticking with the more careless and dishonoring behaviors that are so common in these interactions? What results do we think we will reap other than an abundance of battles while love between us diminishes? And how do we think this will affect our children? Our friends? Our business associates? And our world?

As we sincerely try to answer these questions it becomes shockingly clear how much easier being nice is than not being nice. So why don't we indulge in the former, rather than the later? And why don't we argue for it, rather than defend slipping out of it? Tom and I think it's because, as simple as this concept is, nobody has previously thought seriously about how powerful it would be to actually begin the process of treating our primary partners with honor on a daily, moment-to-moment basis.

But once we have thought of it, the only thing that makes sense is for each of us to begin *now* to practice the loving kindness we consistently claim to value whenever asked about what counts most in life. So rather than hold loving each other as an ideal we practice only occasionally, we suggest each of us get out of the starter's gate and begin now to act on this goal.

Could it be that this simple switch in the way we view things and behave in our homes is the key to a rapidly better world? We suggest that you and your husband stop debating the topic and simply begin. What harm can it do it give it a try? But the key is that you each decide to make it your own project and monitor yourself, rather than the other. This is how to not only stop new battles over this new idea, but guarantee your own success.

We wish you well in this new and joyful endeavor and hope you will let us know how it works for you.

Tom says: I agree with Bobbie. Your husband has raised an important question frequently asked in a variety of ways in our *Settle for More* seminars and therapy sessions.

—"Do you really do as you say?"

—"Isn't it easier for you two because you are therapists (implying that unless you have some mystical requisite skills, you could not possibly hold to a higher standard)?"

—"How can you expect anyone to be nice all of the time?"

—"I'm only human, aren't I?"

While people phrase the questions differently, they are variations on the same theme: a search for a reason for not being able/not wanting to raise the bar on their expectations for relationships AND on how they will be in those relationships. To put it another way, those posing the questions are looking for a way to explain and thus justify continuing what they are doing in the face of knowing that it is not working.

Our responses to these questions are: Yes. No. We can't. Yes you are, so what?

Yes, Bobbie and I have committed to a standard that we feel is consistent with and will give us the relationship in which we want to be. Do we always reach that standard? No. But there are only occasional lapses and those are becoming quite scarce. If your husband feels the standard we espouse is too high, then what standard does he subscribe to and can he articulate it? Will it give him the relationship he wants? More importantly, will it give you the relationship you want?

No, it is not easier for us because we are therapists. Articulating and then setting a standard that guaranteed we would have and keep the relationship we wanted to be in did not require any particular skill set. It required that we realize the importance of the relationship, our desire to make it work and our commitment to do whatever it takes. We know what we want, we are fully aware of the cultural pull to settle for less, and are committed to swimming against that cultural tide. It takes no more than that. By the sound of his question, your husband appears capable of understanding the difference between settling for less and settling for more. Tell him it is a matter of choice, not training. The success couples have had with this model attests to its universality. Ask him to make the choice.

We can't expect anyone to be anything. However, given that I have articulated completely, openly and unequivocally to Bobbie the kind of relationship I want to be in, I do expect my behavior to be consistent with that. Being nice to the person I love and want to share my life with is consistent with that expectation. And why would I be anything else? If you can come up with a reason, it is just that ... an excuse for poor behavior. Anything less than "being nice" is a guarantee to put a tear in the fabric of the relationship and takes a little nick out of the heart of our partner. One nick may not do much, but enough of them and scar tissue will form, increasing the risk of relationship failure. So, do we expect people to be nice all the time? No. But I really wonder why they would not be nice to the person they say they love and want to be loved by. Maybe your husband can come up with something that makes sense. If he does, please let us know.

Yes, you and your husband are only human, but I don't know what that has to do with raising the bar on what you will accept in your relationship. What distinguishes humans from lower-order animals is our capacity for abstract thinking and the ability to reason and make the choices that will serve ourselves and our partners. We are not just stimulus-response machines with no ability to override impulses.

Being human is an asset, not a liability. Our failing has been that we have used our humanness as an excuse rather than to call upon ourselves to live up to our capacities in our relationships with all animals, including humans. So, yes we are only human. And if your husband is using this as an excuse, blow him a raspberry and tell him your expectation in your relationships is that he will act like one and not like the lower-order animals.

And as Bobbie so eloquently stated, this is actually the only hope for successful relationships—all relationships. It has been clearly demonstrated, as Bobbie pointed, out that being nice to others not only has a positive effect on the recipient of the nicety but on anyone who witnesses the act. The obverse is also true; people feel badly when we are not nice, both the recipient of the bad behavior and those who observe it. Here is the point: The shape of my relationship shapes my world.

Bobbie and I invite you and your husband to set your standards so that they allow you to shape a positive, loving relationship and then enjoy it—and the shape of the world you have created.

◉ Stop The Train !

Dear Tom & Bobbie,

I have been reading your column regularly and have tried to follow some of the advice you have given but it doesn't seem to work with this problem. My partner and I fight a lot and he seems to enjoy it. It looks to me as if he tries to goad me into fights. If I remain neutral and "come from my heart" as you have recommended in one of your columns, he just presses harder, looking for something to hook me until I fire back, and then we are off to the races. So, that is one part of it. But what I am really having difficulty with is that when he has had enough of the battle he just stops and then wants to make up and be sexual. At this point, the last thing I want is to have sex with him. But if I do not, he will pout and then get angry again. We have repeated this pattern countless times and nothing ever really gets solved. I want to stop it. What can I do?

Tom says: Stop the train now! Either get it onto a different track or get off the train. Because the way the two of you interact is guaranteed to perpetuate the difficulties you have described and you are headed for a disastrous relationship wreck.

While there are many possible reasons why your partner defaults to this unpleasant behavior, he sounds like someone who engages you through fighting and confuses this with intimacy and will only experience the relationship as successful after you have slugged it out and then made up. Thinking that this is at the least strange and at the most sick behavior, you might believe all you need do is let him know that what he is doing is dishonoring, unloving, destructive, selfish and guaranteed damaging to the loving feelings you once held for him, and with this information he would immediately stop. You probably have said this or some variation there of plus, and nothing has happened. And it won't because this is just fuel for the argument fire.

If there is one thing that has been demonstrated repeatedly in the area of psychology it is: Reward the behavior you want to continue and ignore the behavior you want to extinguish. This works with children, adolescents, bosses—everyone.

When behavior persists it is because there is a payoff. So, despite your requests that your partner do things differently, until you find out what the payoff is for him and remove it, he will continue the let's-fight-let's-have-sex cycle. We can't know all of the nuances of your situation but from what you say, there are two areas where it appears you are providing the payoff to your intimacy impaired partner. First, if he were not able to "hook" you, there would be no argument. So, suggestion #1 is don't take the bait. Simply decline to engage in that sort of conversation.

But the big payoff that keeps the cycle going is the after-argument sex. Ramping up his adversarial interaction until you jump into the argument is his foreplay. It gets him the false sense of intimacy when you give in to the sex. As long as you ultimately say "yes" you are guaranteed of seeing more his unwanted behavior. You are in affect training him to be the person you say you do not want.

So, in answer to your question, "what can I do?" the answer does not lie in "doing" anything. Rather it is to stop doing. Stop engaging when he initiates the fighting and stop giving in to his sexual demands. Find a time when things are relatively peaceful and in a side-by-side conversation tell him directly that you are going to ignore both his invitations to fight and the requests for sex that follow. And then follow through. If he continues the press for both despite your remaining detached, remove yourself. If you do not follow through, you need to assess what the payoff is for you to keep it going.

This will put a temporary halt to his junk. But it will not solve the underlying issues that are the genesis of the destructive interaction you both are engaged in. If his behaviors continue then get professional help to get the train on a different track. Or get off. Either way, the ultimate goal is to change the direction of the train and have it headed towards a positive healthy relation ship that benefits both of you.

Bobbie says: I wholeheartedly agree and would add two more points. Like you seem to be doing, many women err in telling men repeatedly that they don't like arguing, but then get stridently engaged in this oppositional form of faux intimacy as well as the highly reinforcing follow-up sex. Instead of getting pulled into this cycle that has the illusion of working for your husband while taking you out of feelings of closeness, you would be wise to more carefully share just how much his oppositional behavior is repelling to you, perhaps even leading to a loss of love for him, as many woman in counseling have shared happens for them. So rather than engage in the fights or fill your head and heart with negative feelings associated with him, give your husband an honest choice between persisting in using this repugnant pattern and trying something new that will lead to genuine intimacy between you.

Tom and Bobbie say: Once this arguing and making-up cycle is out of the way, we would suggest that both of you fill the vacuum created by more actively seeking positive ways to relate to each other ... and in doing this to consider our goal of focusing on how you can *settle for more*, rather than the *less* your constant arguing is now creating for you. Good luck and let us know how it turns out.

🌑 Actively Frustrated

Dear Tom and Bobbie

My partner and I were told that if we wanted to avoid arguments and improve our relationship we should learn the skills of "active listening." We tried it. It doesn't work. I just get frustrated and we end up arguing about how to do the active listening steps. Is there something else we can do or should we just avoid sensitive topics.

Tom says: Many have been told if they wish to improve their relationship, they need to listen better. They are given practice exercises in order to "do" better listening and like you, are surprised and become frustrated when they try to use these newly learned skills in topic-sensitive conversations. They find that in spite of these new tools, temperatures continue to rise, along with the volume, until they are dug into their respective foxholes lobbing incoming rounds at each other.

So why doesn't it work? Because we have been asking the wrong question. Rather than ask, "What can *we do*," and then launch into some newly learned behaviors, we need to ask, "How do *I* need to *be* for things to change?"

When we alter how we are *being*, what we *do* will also be different and if it is not, it is out of alignment with who we want to **be** and becomes immediately evident. Without this change in context, or change in the way we are *being*, any behavioral changes will be clumsy and temporary—often surviving for only a few minutes—before we revert back to our old, unsuccessful ways of getting our point across, and the war is on.

Now, this might sound like a lot of psychobabble. Half right. It is based on psychological principles, but it is not babble. It works. And here's how.

First, and perhaps most difficult, we need to ask the questions: How do I want to *be* in this relationship? Do I really *want* this relationship to work? Do I really *want* to stop the fighting? Am I willing to come from a place of understanding my partner that eliminates the need to argue?

Search your heart and answer these questions coming from that place of who you *are* and how you want to *be*. If the answer is yes to each question, you are in a position to transform your relationship in a way you may not have thought possible. You are now in a place to practice the art of *active understanding* as opposed to active listening.

The difference between the two is not so much in the how we *do* it, but in the how we are *being* someone who wants to understand. If understanding is used as one of the measures of success in my relationship, rather than being right, the need to argue is automatically eliminated. Thus the moment I commit to being the understander, the environment for communication has drastically shifted.

Now when Bobbie and I have points of view that seem to differ, I no longer need to do my best to convince her that I am right and she is incorrect or wrong ... and there is no need for her to defend herself. With active understanding, my goal is to understand her story and once done, hers is to understand mine. This allows us to get to a larger, more expanded third story that includes all or parts of *both* of our viewpoints.

When it seems we are beginning to disagree, we do not let things slide into the old agree-to-disagree way of solving our differences. Rather we actively go after understanding each other and the larger third story.

And why wouldn't I do this with Bobbie? She is bright, sharp and has done very well in the thinking department throughout her life without any help from me. So, if she has a point of view that differs from mine, I not only respect it, but I want to know how she got there. I want to *understand*.

Two things are important here. First, I respect my partner. Second, there is never only one point of view. There are a number of points of view about any subject and a number of ways to do or see things that have as much validity as mine.

If I think my point of view is the only valid or *right* one, then I am either God or delusional. And if I think I am the former, I am the latter.

To discount my partner discounts the relationship and the person I say I honor, respect, cherish and want to spend the rest of my life with. Why would I do that?

If I insist on my way or point of view, I am seriously limiting the possibilities of my relationship. When I fully explore my partner's thoughts, while listening without debating, I will often find that we do not disagree at all. And out of my understanding her and her understanding me, we develop a third story. And this has never failed us. We have *always* been able to get to the third story. So, become a co-author of the third stories in your relationship. They make wonderful day-to-day reading.

☻ Ambivalent

Dear Tom and Bobbie,

In a recent column you talked about relationships that are not good enough to stay in yet not bad enough to leave. You are describing my very unhappy 15 year marriage that my friends think I should leave. Why is it so hard for me to face this?

Bobbie says: If we are in partnerships filled with both good and bad, we get confused. This is because the good times tend to dissolve the pain of the bad ones they follow and cause us to perpetually view each good phase as a fresh start with new hope. This pattern gets us hooked, often even addicted, to this back and forth arrangement coupled with our effort to "get through" to our partner in hopes they will change. To get out of the trap we must look at the relationship in its entirety as something filled with more bad than we should tolerate, rather than compartmentalized in a way that allows us to inappropriately adapt to the bad times.

To get out of this never-ending cycle that friends can see is not leading to happiness, we must look at the relationship in its entirety as something often filled with far more bad times than we should tolerate. By doing this we stop compartmentalizing the bad times into smaller, more manageable segments. Once we face that the full experience is less tolerable than we realized and the pattern is not going to resolve itself, we realize we must seek outside help to change it or help us leave. So if you are serious about interrupting this pattern one direction or another, you would be wise to seek intervention.

Tom says: I have a little different slant on the problem you present. Without any more information it is difficult to answer why you have such ambivalence about facing and dealing with your situation. Is this the only area of your life in which you are ambivalent? If so then you are asking the correct question. Many who remain in no-hope relationships find it difficult to confront and deal with problems in other areas of their lives as well. If you fall into this camp then you most likely have adopted a way of dealing with life problems that simply does not serve you well and the issue is much larger than simply dealing with your marriage which is no small feat in itself.

Assuming you are doing well and handling all the other speed bumps of life I would want to know what the pay off is in maintaining the relationship status quo? It may not be readily apparent to you, but there *is* a pay off. You have been married for 15 years and were probably together for some time before that so you have a significant amount of your life invested in something that your friends think you should leave. A side note here: Friends can give us valuable feedback to help us see situation. But that is all it is. It is your relationship and you are the one who lives with the consequences of your decision, not your friends.

So, I suggest you do some self-checking and identify specifically what keeps you there. Financial and/or physical security? Companionship-as bad as it may be? Sex? Status? The feeling of being needed? Belief that no matter what, you should stay in a marriage? Shame and/or guilt? The devil you know is better than the devil you don't? (to mention a few of the possibilities.)

Whatever the reasons, you need to examine them closely. Because then and only then can you make the decision of whether the cost to you in terms of your health, happiness, and sense of self is worth continuing on. Without understanding why you remain in the relationship you will be unable to make the appropriate get-in-or-get-out decision.

● Boys' Night Out

Dear Bobbie and Tom,

There's an ad on television showing a group of men singing joyfully about "Boys' Night Out" that caused a big fight between my husband and me. As we got into it, he made me feel I am an obstacle to his "living" life with the kind of freedom and joy he had before marriage and children. In fact, I got so heated up after our fight that I asked him to take a permanent "boys' night out." He can't believe I want to get a divorce over this and says he wants to stay married. Nobody is more shocked than I am. What's up that he seems to want to get away from me, but then have me here waiting when he gets home? I want a relationship with a more mature man who truly wants to do what he said he wanted when we were courting ... to share his life with me.

Bobbie says: This is an excellent question that quickly exposes some of the cultural attitudes that undermine positive feelings toward women along with our potential for enjoying truly wonderful partnerships.

This is because, as silly as it is, the ad fairly accurately reflects our cultural attitude toward our primary relationships following marriage and serves as an exaggerated caricature of how we behave in a manner during courtship that is very different from the way we behave once we are married.

In fact, the pervasive cultural attitude perpetuated by these ads in conjunction with a plethora of sitcoms, movies, and plays showing married couples sniping at each other is that relationships become more of a nuisance than a source of fulfillment of our very real desire for enduring love and happiness.

And so we find ourselves laughing over wanting to get away from the very thing the majority of people dream most intensely about having ... a loving, supportive and joyful partnership. Yet, because the humor is based on lost dreams, it masks the disappointment so many people honestly feel, and statistics tell us that these kinds of attitudes may entertain us, but they also fail to fulfill us. The question is, how do we get from being madly in love in our primary partnerships to wanting a "boys' night out"?

In many cases, husbands are the ones who first view marriage as a "completed task," and once the challenge of winning their wives' hearts has been accomplished, they return to the lives they were living before they met and married them.

Women are less likely to see it this way and at first resist this shift in the relationship and strive to draw their husbands back into the wonderful "courtship" mode that attracted them to each other in the first place.

Unfortunately, the wives' efforts to return to earlier levels of love and caring sound like complaints to their husbands who in turn respond defensively. Wives may then turn up the volume on their requests and a battle between them is underway. This battle is then met with even more distancing with wives feeling abandoned and left with hard choices while husbands are not fulfilled in the midst of such a battleground. Both seek ways to deal with the bewilderment and hurt of love slipping away and may express their frustration by pouting and withdrawing or getting overtly angry and combative. But the end result is a growing band of distance between them, and over time, each looks to other people and activities for a sense of the connection they originally sought in each other.

The frustration for those who start their partnerships in this way is that they are fraught with disappointment and friction, not the kinds of emotions either party thought they were signing up for.

I watched my husband consciously choose not to go down this fruitless road, and by this choice I have felt continuously honored by him and free from the disappointments, anger and nagging so many women experience when their husbands default without awareness to the culturally paved road we see reflected in the "boys' night out" ad.

Once this dishonoring road is by-passed, so are many of the problems of marriage as we know them in today's world. But even more important, the alternate road leads to new possibilities for truly wonderful and loving partnerships.

Tom says: Ads, sitcoms, novels—all those forms of media that depict relationships in caricature do so because they sell. And these messages of relationship mediocrity become our primary source of relationship modeling. As such, they have tremendous impact on the form and quality of the relationships in our culture.

Given that most of us had limited models of successful relationships to learn from in our developmental years (after all, our parents' didn't have any better sources of information and modeling than we did) I am not surprised people adopt wholesale the models of relationship provided by the popular media.

From infancy through adolescence to our gerontological winding down, we are the recipients of nonstop messages about the way relationships are, what we can anticipate from them and the behavior that is expected. Bevis and Butthead, the Simpsons, Ray Romano, Jennifer Lopez, Phyllis Diller, Jackie Collins (author of The Bitch and The Stud) etc., become cultural relationship gurus explicitly and implicitly giving their followers the mantra: "Thou shall dishonor thy partner."

I have done that. I have been relationship stupid. If I had been able to sit back and view myself objectively, I would have come to the conclusion that my thinking was disordered because I would have seen that my behavior was guaranteed to not get me what I wanted. And what I want is a permanent, wonderful, ever expanding partnership.

So, how does all of this relate to your quandary? While you have not given us any information on what you might have contributed to the relationship waltz you and your husband are doing, what you say about your partner is that he is clearly manifesting relationship-stupid symptoms with a poor prognosis; in particular is the cultural myth that goes something like this: I was a successful, active person before I met you. We met and dated. I fell in love with you and you with me. We married. Now I can carry on with my pre-marital successful-active behaviors AND do marriage and live happily ever after.

I would bet that when believers in this myth are challenged by their partners to change their behavior so that it is more in line with the way they had been in the courting premarital period, their responses would include, "Why should I have to give up (fill in the blank here with whatever behavior it is that is the focus of the request) to make the relationship work?" I wonder if those who take this position realize how utterly stupid it sounds?

Think about it: "I know that the way I behaved before we married is what attracted my partner to me. Now that we are married, I am going to stop doing those things I know that will keep her attracted to me—and complain about it." Sounds somewhat below the level of thinking that goes with single digit IQ's.

It would be like going to a car dealer, saying I want that car, agreeing to the car payments and then once I drive the car home complaining about having to pay for that damn car. When I buy a car, I do not complain about losing the money, I brag about, take care of and show off my car. I can't have both my money and my car. I have to make a choice. And the choice is easy. I do not have to "give up" my money or "sacrifice" anything. I have what I want and am pleased. If I am not, then I should be a pedestrian. Life would be a lot simpler.

It is my experience and I think Bobbie would concur that in general, you cannot revert back to premarital, single behavior and expect to have your partnership thrive—or survive.

Given the paucity of cultural support for the notion that you can have a partnership of unlimited possibilities, one that continues to grow and expand AFTER the marriage, it is understandable that many males will opt to operate in the automobile model. The purveyors of relationship pap in conjunction with our own familial histories makes a very tough, if not impossible, sale of the notion that being on our good behavior after the marriage is guaranteed to get us what we want.

What it seems to require is a leap of faith. I have taken the leap and can tell you that it works. Are there set backs? Rough spots? Periods of doubt? Sure. But staying in the model we propose allows for resolution of these relationship speed bumps and experiencing what we all want: an ever expanding, exhilarating positive partnership.

◐ Still Searching for Happiness

Dear Bobbie and Tom,

I am very unhappy in my relationship, but my friends think I should "get real" and be satisfied with what I have as they have done. Although they admit they are not particularly happy, they no longer feel as actively unhappy as I do. Is this the best way to deal with marital disappointment and return to more happiness?

Bobbie says: No, it's not. Talking ourselves into feeling satisfied with lost dreams and unmet goals offers a "faux fix" approach to accommodating life's disappointments.

By lowering our standards to align with our results, we hope to trick the mind into not feeling so actively frustrated by the way things have turned out.

Although I used to engage in this "cooking the books" approach to feeling happy, I now view the illusion achieved as one of our greatest cultural errors, since by doing this we are progressively *settling for less* in increasingly more of the arenas of our lives.

As a result, restaurants and stores offer us less value for more cost, the substance of our movies and media is often substandard, and many other business and service industries are not fulfilling their promises. In addition jobs are often unrewarding, the quality of schools is rapidly declining, and stats show that our relationships with partners—and others—fail more often than they succeed. This cultural habit of *settling for less* is cumulatively bringing less to our lives, our hearts, and our humanity. We then respond by complaining about our losses or trying to repair the pain in haphazard spurts. Yet we know in our hearts that this cultural habit of *settling for less* is at the core of what's not working.

I was recently blessed with the concept that rather than continue down this barren road, I could actually have *more* in my life, an idea that came to my awareness the day I bumped into Tom. We had enjoyed brief mutual crushes in the 8th grade, but then went our separate ways into other marriages, careers, kids, and grandkids. However when we reunited in our later

years, we fell deeply in love and had the wisdom at that juncture to cherish what we had found.

Yet others kept predicting that it couldn't possibly endure
and urged us to enjoy it while it lasted. Some even seemed to
wait eagerly for our love to cool off so we would rejoin them in
settling into the LESS that so many have come to accept as
"normal."

This reserved response to our great joy served as an inadver-
tent blessing, since it awakened in us the idea that we did not
have to slip into this culturally normalized expectation of This
cultural habit of *settling for less*. Instead we agreed to stay awake
to our love and to consciously be and do the things needed to
keep it alive. In short, we agreed *not lower the bar*, but to raise
it, and in doing so to *settle for more* rather than *less*.

As soon as we made this decision, we became more conscious of the feelings and attitudes that fed our love and those
that could undermine it. As a result, any time we began to slip
into old habits destined to destroy the positive feelings
between us, we stopped ourselves and discussed it. We then
replaced these destructive pathways with alternate ideas and
possibilities.

To our surprise, we benefited from our new course even
more than we had expected. In fact we noticed that our love
not only failed to diminish, but was growing deeper and
stronger.

Doing this proved to us that nobody needs to *settle for less*
as a way to by-pass feelings of disappointment and live a life of
pretend happiness. So we decided to teach others how to join
us in by-passing this culturally paved road that leads to flattened feelings rather than genuine aliveness and joy.

Thus, I would suggest that you too, hold onto your hope
and stick with your instinct to *settle for more*.

Help your husband to understand that the source of his own
discontent starts with his willingness to *settle for less* in what he

offers your relationship and ask him to join you on this very different road of *settling for more.*

If you need outside help to support you in getting there, then find it. If your husband doesn't want to play life in the *settling for more* lane, he may not be the right person for you.

Good luck to both of you in uncovering what you want and then keeping the faith that you can get there.

● My Husbands Attitude Is Making Me Crazy

Dear Bobbie and Tom,

We've been married for 7 years and have a 4 and 6 year old. My husband started a new job and insists he has to go out dancing after training sessions with a mixed group of younger colleagues. When I object he tells me I'm a shrew and have no right to tell him what to do. But it's making me crazy and I have no clue how to solve this. Can you help?

Bobbie says: Your question indicates that your husband is behaving in a way that fails to show you the kind of love and honoring you want to experience in your primary partnership. It also suggests that your attempt to let him know how this affects you is not of interest to him. So stop trying to convince him how he should behave as so many women erroneously spend years trying to do. Falling into this trap of scolding and then feeling crazed due to a lack of responsiveness on his part will indeed make you the villain he says you are—and an old and increasingly loud one at that, if you continue doing this for another ten years.

In addition, by putting so much energy into pushing him to be someone different than he is, you are not facing who is really there living with you and asking yourself whether or not you want to invest your precious adult life in this questionable experience.

So I suggest you take your husband's advice and stop telling him what to do. Begin, instead, to work only on yourself. Start by taking all of your own "stuff" that does not support wonderful partnership off the table, including yelling and scolding.

Then begin to more carefully observe, rather than resist, the design for partnership your husband comes up with on his own. Remain friendly yet give him honest feedback. For example, let him know that his desire to go out dancing with others, combined with his unwillingness to discuss the impact of this on your heart and relationship, is more repelling than attractive to you. But only mention this once so that he has the benefit of your truth, without you using the information to "push" him to be different or motivate him to change. In other words, trust what Maya Angelou says when she offers, "When someone shows you who they are, believe them."

If you do these simple things, it will soon be crystal clear whether you are in a relationship filled with unlimited possibilities or one that offers you only one option of *settling for less* rather than *more*.

Tom says: Couldn't agree more with Bobbie. Your husband sounds like so many partners who break from the gate with a lot of strength, showing you in the courting phase how neat they are. And then after the marriage they show you who they really are. This comes from a basic lack of understanding what it takes to build the kind of relationship you want to be in for the long haul. Thinking that the purpose of dating is to "get and have" a partner, he is into a "me-vs.-you" view of relationships as opposed to a "we" perspective, reflecting a self centered way of thinking and a need to win in any and all arguments. The need for immediate gratification, his I-should-be-able-to-have-and-do-what-I-want point of view, the nanny-nanny-boo-boo flavor to his name calling and his lack of interest and caring for the other suggest that he is still operating socially and interpersonally in a very adolescent mode, and early adolescence at that.

Name calling and dishonoring language as opposed to side-by-side conversations at the least are a sign that he feels his perceived "rights" are more important than the relationship. At the worst they suggest he does not care about the relationship and in fact may have moved on. And you need to find out where this kid is on the continuum.

You do have every "right" to let him know the kind of relationship you want to be in. And as Bobbie has suggested I would take the opportunity to do just that. In doing so he will know what you want but more importantly, by hearing what he wants you will be able to see how he views relationships. Does he want a nurturing, supportive and honoring relationship where the "we" is important or does he want an adolescent partnership based on "me" and "my" wants and needs? With this information in hand you can then make a choice: We hope you will Settle for More.

◉ No Way Out

Dear Tom and Barbie,

My 8-year marriage feels as if it is circling the drain. We argue constantly. She says I've changed and is not sure she likes the "new" me. I think she is the one who has changed into a nagging shrew. We have been seeing a marriage counselor who tells me that I need to overlook my wife's nastiness and try harder to make it work. While I would love to get back to what we had at first, the way she is makes it impossible. I just do not want to keep doing the same thing and getting the same result. Nothing. What can I do to get her to at least be civil? If she won't change, should I bail?

Tom says: Relationships that have reached the make-break point such as yours are painful and certainly not what we signed up for when we said, "I do." However, while it might not seem possible, there are more than the two options of "either change or I leave" that you present, and my suggestion is that you explore them.

How did the relationship get to where it is today? Did you wake up one morning and find yourself married to a stranger, someone different than the one you lovingly kissed goodnight the evening before? I doubt it.

Most likely it developed slowly, though certainly, over the full eight years. And my hunch is you had a lot to do with that development.

Marriage is a team sport with only one team. No one has to lose for your team to win. However, you do have to agree on how you are going to keep score and what will constitute a win.

In situations such as yours, partners will point to the other and say it would all be ok if *YOU* would change. This does not usually prove to be all that helpful. And as you describe your situation, you have not been very successful with this tact in altering your wife's behaviors. You will be no more successful as her behavior-boss than she has been as yours.

But you can change your own behavior ... in fact this is the only thing you can change. So, I suggest you seriously look at your contribution to the team's win/loss record, and what you describe as the possible end of the team's franchise.

Granted, you have got your hands full! But one very quick way to lighten your load would be for you to pay attention to how much of the responsibility for the relationship going south is attributable to your behavior.

A good way to do this is to ask yourself, "If I saw someone in a relationship acting the way I have been acting, no matter what the reason, would that be someone I would like to be married to?"

When you get a clear picture of your own behavior from this perspective as a witness, see if you can honestly say that it honors your partner, is respectful, honest, open and loving. Is it truly the way you want to be in a relationship? If not, take note of which of your attitudes and behaviors you would find repelling because you now have an opportunity and the blue print to put your relationship back on track.

How? You have just identified what you are doing that is guaranteed for you to *not* get what you want ... assuming that what you do want is a successful relationship with your partner.

So, stop doing those things you found unattractive in your self-inventory, and take them completely off the table. This allows her to not have to *react* to **your** "stuff," and all that is left is **hers**.

It is a two-step process, however. Pulling back may give temporary relief but will not do a thing for the long term health of the relationship.

The second step requires that you replace your relationship-busting behaviors with those things that made your partner fall in love with you in the first place. The good news is that this is easy. You have already demonstrated that you can do it. There's nothing new to learn.

So you can keep doing what you're doing and the outcome will be predictable. But our thought is, if what you are doing isn't working, stop doing it ... and things will change. Guaranteed. At the least, you will know that you did all you could.

At best this simple two-step process over which you have complete control, may transform your relationship. And your partner may very well return to the behaviors and a way of being that made you fall in love with her some eight years ago.

If you and your wife decide this is what you want, that this is the kind of relationship in which you want to be, then the two-step process can get, and keep you there. Just remember, you are on the same team. Our hope is that you will be celebrating your joint win.

◔ Don't Be a Dodo

Dear Bobbie and Tom,

My partner and I have been together for three years and are in a committed monogamous relationship, one in which we trust and respect each other. However, he is an attractive, very out-going man who my friends find "interesting," so much so that several of them have hit on him at parties. I have pointed this out to him on two different occasions and he got very defensive, stating categorically that it had not happened and that I must be making it up, inferring that I am paranoid. I am not making it up and I am not paranoid. I don't understand why he can't see it. I can't bring it up any more without getting into a fight. I do not know how to get him to understand how I feel this seriously threatens our relationship. Help.

Tom says: The two of you are seeing this from very different viewpoints ... which doesn't need to be a deal breaker. It will be, however, if either one of you fails to understand the other's take. Here's how you might avoid that outcome.

Your partner's response suggests several possibilities.

First, he is a player. He knows full well that he is being hit on—could, in fact, actually be encouraging it—and may be carrying on some extra curricular activities when you are not looking.

Second, he knows it is going on. He enjoys the attention but has no intention of taking the interaction any further than party-time flirting.

If he falls into either of these possibilities, you need to decide whether you want to be in a relationship that is not honoring, one in which you are diminished and discounted. If you do not want to be in this kind of relationship, then confront the issue directly. Let him know that his behavior is not what you signed up for and your feelings are non-negotiable. If he wants to continue acting this way, honor his position, and get out of a relationship that appears to have a fatal flaw.

A third explanation is that he is simply a social dodo. He is totally unconscious to the behavior of your friends. This is the most probable explanation for his reaction to your concerns—assuming your description of your relationship is accurate.

If this is the case, there is good news and bad news. The good news is that the chances are very good that he will be able to expand his awareness and understand your concerns. The bad news is he is a social dodo. There is a good reason the dodo bird is extinct—it simply was not able to adapt to a threatening environment. So, while your partner may understand your concerns, unless he truly wants to be in an honoring relationship, his dishonoring and marginalizing behaviors will continue. And my hunch is this will make your relationship with him extinct.

Finally, the fact that he is unconscious to the hustling of your "friends" seems to be a genetic anomaly in a great many males. However, this can and should not be an excuse for his behavior once he is alerted. If, after you try to approach him in a side-by-side conversation, he continues with the denial that is part of a dodo's behavior, ask him to read this column. When he understands the dynamic and the discomfort and anguish it causes you, he has a choice: honor and support you and do everything possible to set limits and boundaries that will stop your friends in their tracks or continue down the path of the dodo.

Bobbie says: You have raised such an important question about this common interaction between a flirting woman and the man she is hitting on that I will comment here and again in our next column on the far-reaching impact these interactions have on partners and partnerships.

In most cases, a woman feels deeply devalued and diminished anytime her partner passively allows another woman to flirt with him, or worse seems to enjoy the attention or perhaps even actively engages in it.

Because these culturally sanctioned flirtations have been promoted as "harmless," partners are expected to be good sports about it, and those who complain are viewed as uptight and insecure or unduly jealous.

Yet as Tommy so aptly points out, the dodos who strive to silence their partners with denials and counter accusations are missing the point. What they are failing to perceive is that their flirtations not only cause their partners to feel deeply hurt and no longer cherished, but to also feel less bonded and connected to them. For many women this marks the beginning of a breakdown in the partnership big enough to threaten its survival, a threat we will discuss further in our next column.

For now suffice it to say, that you are not "crazy" to feel as you do, nor are the many other women who don't want flirtations to be a part of their partnership experience. In addition to the information I have gathered on flirtation during my thirty years of listening to women hurt by it, I would like to invite readers, both men and women, to share their experiences and views as we continue to address this important topic.

Meanwhile, I would encourage you, as you consider the various components you want in your partnership, to use as your guide your own commitment to settle for more.

⬤ The Larger Impact of Flirtations

Dear Tom and Bobbie,

My husband thinks I'm a flirt and doesn't trust me to go out with men from the office for business lunches. I have always enjoyed "harmless" flirtations, but he hasn't felt they were as meaningless as I have assumed them to be. More recently he has started flirting to make his point, and I must confess I don't like it. Now I'm beginning to wonder if flirting is really as okay as most people seem to think or if we're both being overly sensitive and jealous.

Bobbie says: Statistics tell us that in 80 percent of all marriages, one or more of the partners has at some point engaged in an affair, suggesting that somewhere between 40-50 percent or more of our partners are involved in some sort of extra-marital activity. We can probably deduce that a flirtation in one form or another preceded most of these encounters, and I would further deduce that our cultural tolerance of these flirtations contributes more than we have realized to the subsequent marital dalliances reported.

In fact, prior to my recently becoming involved with the concept that we can *settle for more* in our relationships if we make a point of highly honoring and tending to our partners and partnerships, I too was lulled into the notion that flirtations are simply a normal and "harmless" part of male-female interactions. And so, rather than be as taken aback by the prevalence of them which now seems a more appropriate reaction, I too was once part of the permissiveness about these activities that are so hurtful to our partners and destructive to our relationships.

I no longer agree with my earlier viewpoint regarding the "harmlessness" of flirtations, since once we pause to look at their true impact on relationships, it becomes instantly clear just how incompatible they are with the goal of honoring our partners and creating good partnerships. And because honoring our partners is the basis for having truly wonderful partnerships, flirting is clearly incompatible with that goal.

So, I would now suggest that anyone who is flirting, stop in their own tracks and ask themselves why they have lost sight of the importance of valuing and honoring their partner. And if your partner is flirting, I would suggest you take an honest inventory of the ongoing purpose of remaining in a relationship in which you are dishonored.

For when we stop to think about it, flirtations are not by their very nature "harmless," since they include stealing our interest, attention and other positive energies away from our partner in order to give these gifts of our hearts to someone else. Not only is this a hurtful betrayal to our partner, it dilutes the intensity of our own feelings for our partners including our sexual feelings. While doing this, we cannot possibly have a successful relationship with our partner, much less an outrageous one. We have already taken ourselves out of our partnership in order to engage in the flirtation. Culturally, we have been kidding ourselves that this can be done, when in fact being in a relationship and being in a flirtation are incompatible. And doing it briefly is not any more "harmless" or values-based than lying for brief periods of time.

This brings us to the question of just when is an interaction with someone from the opposite sex a flirtation? I think we all know in our hearts when we are offering a person that extra charge of animated male-female energy, as we put our most charming foot forward that we no longer give so steadily to our partner. Although much of this can be done energetically and invisibly, including the exchange of sexual energy, some of the bleed-through outer manifestations include things like frequent glances, extended eye contact, touching, and perhaps even caressing the other person in some way, while keeping the verbal communication going exclusively between us.

So, back to the question, is this "harmless?" Once we put this topic on the table and begin asking, it's clear that it's not. So we are going to lead the way in asking people to reconsider their views on this commonly accepted activity and the impact it has on their partners and partnerships. Please share yours with us at Merrill@lava.net. And always remember, you can *settle for more.*

Tom says: This is a variation on our column last week in which we addressed the *flirtee.* Your question however deals with the *flirter.* I agree completely with Bobbie's take on this, so no need to cover the same ground. However, I think it important to consider who is being affected by the "harmless" flirtations when trying to determine if in fact it is. The affect that your flirting has on you and your partner is your business. And if you were the only two who were touched by the behavior and you want to continue, have at it! But you are not. You are also making a significant impact on the *flirtee* and his or her relationship.

There are some wonderful studies that demonstrate the affect our behavior has on the emotional well being and behaviors of those who see or are touched by it ... and the affect they then have on those who see or are touched by them ... and so on. It is like a pebble thrown into a calm lake with the ripples moving out over the glassy body of water, not stopping until they reach the shore in all directions.

Think about it. You flirt with someone who is a relationship. How does that affect their partner? What happens to that relationship? And what affect does that relationship then have on those around it: children, colleagues, friends? And what about those who witness your behavior? How do they feel and what are they thinking? Do they now have to align themselves with one party or another or can they play the "it's harmless" cop-out game? How does it affect their behavior with others in their lives?

It is not harmless. It is incredibly damaging, impacting the lives of others in ways you can not imagine. We can because we deal with the results in our therapy practice. When you are the *flirter*, you are throwing a handful of pebbles into the relationship lake. And you can never take the ripples back.

So, your choice. *Settle for More* or *Settle for less*.

And we leave you with this:

꒰⧖꒱

"Life is very short and there's no time for fussing and fighting." —JOHN LENNON

Advance Praise

SETTLE FOR MORE is an inspired book and I cannot overstate the value of it for anyone who wants to be in a successful relationship. It is a must-read for all who seek to achieve this goal.

Dr. Robert Schuller
Crystal Cathedral Ministries "Hour of of Power"

In clear, understandable terms the authors impart the wisdom and effectiveness of a methodology that has saved thousands of marriages, and improved countless others. This book is must reading for everyone who is married, divorced, or contemplating marriage, as well as for professional marriage counselors who want to greatly improve their skills.

Nicholas A. Cummings, PhD, ScD
Distinguished Professor, University of Nevada, Reno
President, Cummings Foundation for Behavioral Health
Former President, American Psychological Association.

An insightful perspective on human relationships that goes far beyond today's chaotic television "free-for-alls." One CAN have a more satisfying and rewarding life, if only one follows Tom and Bobbie's guiding principle of unconditional respect for others. Their no nonsense vision will make a dramatic difference.

Pat De Leon, PhD
former APA President

It's time marriage has a new belief system ... here it is. It is dedicated to making love work.

Mark Victor Hansen, Co-creator,
#1 New York Times best selling series *Chicken Soup for the Soul*®
Co-author, *The One Minute Millionaire*

This is a book about engaging 100% in the love of life by living a life of love, and Oh!—the rewards to those who decide to engage!

Dr. Elisabet Sahtouris, PhD
Biologist, Speaker, Consultant